EMBELLISHED OPERA ARIAS

RECENT RESEARCHES IN THE MUSIC OF THE NINETEENTH AND EARLY TWENTIETH CENTURIES

Rufus Hallmark and D. Kern Holoman, general editors

A-R Editions, Inc., publishes seven series of musicological editions
that present music brought to light in the course of current research:

Recent Researches in the Music of the Middle Ages and Early Renaissance
Charles Atkinson, general editor

Recent Researches in the Music of the Renaissance
James Haar, general editor

Recent Researches in the Music of the Baroque Era
Christoph Wolff, general editor

Recent Researches in the Music of the Classical Era
Eugene K. Wolf, general editor

Recent Researches in the Music of the Nineteenth and Early Twentieth Centuries
Rufus Hallmark and D. Kern Holoman, general editors

Recent Researches in American Music
H. Wiley Hitchcock, general editor

Recent Researches in the Oral Traditions of Music
Philip V. Bohlman, general editor

Each *Recent Researches* edition is devoted to works
by a single composer or to a single genre of composition.
The contents are chosen for their potential interest to scholars
and performers, then prepared for publication according to the
standards that govern the making of all reliable historical editions.

Subscribers to any of these series, as well as patrons of subscribing institutions,
are invited to apply for information about the "Copyright-Sharing Policy"
of A-R Editions, Inc., under which policy any part of an edition
may be reproduced free of charge for study or performance.

Address correspondence to

A-R EDITIONS, INC.
801 Deming Way
Madison, Wisconsin 53717

RECENT RESEARCHES IN THE MUSIC OF THE NINETEENTH
AND EARLY TWENTIETH CENTURIES • VOLUMES VII AND VIII

EMBELLISHED OPERA ARIAS

Edited by Austin B. Caswell

A-R EDITIONS, INC. • MADISON

© 1989 by A-R Editions, Inc.
All rights reserved
Printed in the United States of America

Library of Congress Cataloging-in-Publication Data

Embellished opera arias.

  1 vocal score.
  (Recent researches in the music of the nineteenth
and early twentieth centuries, ISSN 0193–5364 ; v. 7–8)
  Acc. arr. for piano.
  French or Italian words, also printed as texts with
English translations on p.
  Edited from printed and ms. sources dating from ca.
1821 to 1900.
  Includes bibliographical references.
  Includes 22 arias, each with embellishments by one or
more of 9 different singers.
  1. Operas—Excerpts—Vocal scores with piano.
2. Embellishment (Vocal music)　I. Caswell, Austin B.
II. Series.
M2.R23834 vol. 7–8　[M1507]　　　　　　89-752941
ISBN 0–89579–240–0

Contents

Preface
   The Repertory   vii
   The Singers   ix
   The Music   x
   Sources   xii
   Editorial Methods   xiv
   Critical Notes   xvi
   Acknowledgments   xxii
   Notes   xxii
Texts and Translations   xxiii
Plates   xxxiii

[1]	Ma la sola *(Beatrice di Tenda)*	Vincenzo Bellini	1
[2]	Ah! non credea mirarti *(La sonnambula)*	Vincenzo Bellini	11
[3]	Come per me sereno *(La sonnambula)*	Vincenzo Bellini	15
[4]	De tous les pays *(Le calife de Bagdad)*	François-Adrien Boieldieu	30
[5]	Comme aux jours *(La dame blanche)*	François-Adrien Boieldieu	44
[6]	Non, je ne veux pas chanter *(Le billet de loterie)*	Nicolas Isouard	54
[7]	En vain j'espère *(Robert le diable)*	Giacomo Meyerbeer	67
[8]	Che soave zeffiretto *(Le nozze di Figaro)*	Wolfgang Amadeus Mozart	83
[9]	Voi che sapete *(Le nozze di Figaro)*	Wolfgang Amadeus Mozart	87
[10]	Dunque io son *(Il barbiere di Siviglia)*	Gioachino Rossini	91
[11]	Ecco ridente in cielo *(Il barbiere di Siviglia)*	Gioachino Rossini	102
[12]	Una voce poco fa *(Il barbiere di Siviglia)*	Gioachino Rossini	105, 116
[13]	Nacqui all'affanno *(La Cenerentola)*	Gioachino Rossini	126
[14]	Di piacer mi balza il cor *(La gazza ladra)*	Gioachino Rossini	137
[15]	Sombre forêt *(Guillaume Tell)*	Gioachino Rossini	148
[16]	Pensa alla patria *(L'italiana in Algeri)*	Gioachino Rossini	152
[17]	Parlar, spiegar *(Mosè in Egitto)*	Gioachino Rossini	162
[18]	"Assisa a piè" *(Otello)*	Gioachino Rossini	173

[19]	Ah, quel giorno ognor rammento (*Semiramide*)	Gioachino Rossini	181
[20]	Du séjour de la lumière (*Le siège de Corinthe*)	Gioachino Rossini	189
[21]	Di tanti palpiti (*Tancredi*)	Gioachino Rossini	197
[22]	Lasciami: non t'ascolto (*Tancredi*)	Gioachino Rossini	211

Preface

It is only recently that traditions of music performance in the nineteenth century have come up for the kind of scholarly attention previously devoted almost exclusively to music of earlier eras.[1] Familiarity with nineteenth-century music tended to be assumed—based on the more or less continuous presence of certain works in the standard repertory and on more or less continuous pedagogical genealogies. Yet evidence of nineteenth-century performance styles provided, for example, by early phonograph recordings has helped to shake that sense of familiarity by making us aware of traditions quite different from what is fashionable today.[2]

The present edition focuses on a different kind of evidence, one no less revealing. Many nineteenth-century performers left detailed specifications of their tastes concerning tempo, rhythm, articulation, and ornamentation in a wide variety of sources—memoirs, performance parts, journalistic criticism, and pedagogical literature. This anthology documents nineteenth-century practice in one aspect of vocal performance: extemporized embellishment as it was applied to twenty-two staples of the Italian and French operatic repertoires by some of the foremost performers and pedagogues of the day, several of whom worked directly with the composers of the works they sang. In six of the arias, embellishments by more than one artist can be compared. Since much of this music remains in the standard repertory today, it is hoped that these embellished arias may serve the interests not only of scholars of nineteenth-century performing traditions but also of singers who wish to consider those traditions in preparing their own performances.

The Repertory

The embellished arias of this anthology have been chosen to reflect the Italian-French traditions of lyric theater in Paris during the first half of the nineteenth century. That most of the repertory is Italian reflects how much Italian opera was heard in what was the operatic capital of Europe. Although the popularity of Italian opera in Paris preceded the arrival of Rossini, his invasion of 1824 heralded a generation of Parisian works that, whether composed by Frenchmen or Italians, represented a fusion of national styles—a fusion bemoaned, in spite of its popular success, by such chauvinist observers as Castil-Blaze:

> Rossini appears, Moses lifts his arms toward heaven, and our enchanted academicians hasten to sing once more, "La victoire est à nous!" You are mistaken, comrades; one should say, "The victory is his! The victory is theirs!" If your theater is national, it is only because of its stones. Norway has given you the spruce, Germany and Italy have given you the operas, perhaps someday you will ask for works from the Illinois or the Kabyles! Your Académie Royale de Musique too much resembles the marketplace in Constantinople or in Algiers, where one sells fabrics from Lyons, furniture from Paris, soap from Marseilles, macaroni from Naples, wine from Malaga and from Jerez, while the natives of the country wear nothing but jackal skins.[3]

Rossini's popularity in Paris preceded his arrival and was based upon performances (in Italian or in French) of earlier works. Moreover, these operas maintained their popularity and were not eclipsed by the ones he wrote after his establishment as the preeminent composer of that city. Foremost among these earlier works was *Il barbiere di Siviglia* (Rome, 1816), whose arias are found more frequently in embellished versions than those of any other nineteenth-century opera. Its popularity throughout the Western world was almost instantaneous, but it was not given in Paris until 1819, some months after it had been heard in New York. From this opera I have included three embellished versions of the duet "Dunque io son" [10], in which, however, only Rosina's part is decorated. Count Almaviva's cavatina "Ecco ridente in cielo" [11] is one of the small number of embellishments to be found for male voices. (A bracketed numeral indicates the position of a given piece within the present anthology.) An entire anthology could be devoted solely to embellishments of Rosina's cavatina "Una voce poco fa" [12]. This aria seems to have been accepted as the optimum vehicle for vocal display, and embellishments of it are found in manuals dating from its day to our own. Its appeal seems to lie in the simplicity of its melodic design as well as in the wit and manipulativeness that its text calls upon the singer to display.

L' italiana in Algeri (Venice, 1813) was the first Rossini opera to be heard in Paris (1817) and is still regularly performed today. Isabella's stirring invocation of patriotism, "Pensa alla patria" [16] from the second act, is well known. *Tancredi*, premiered in the same city and same year (Venice, 1813), created Rossini's worldwide reputation. It was first heard in Paris in 1822 and remained in the repertory of the Théâtre-Italien until 1862. Two arias in this anthology are drawn from this opera. The second-act duet between Tancredi and Amenaide, "Lasciami: non t'ascolto" [22], contains ornamentation from two different sources for both roles. Tancredi's cavatina "Di tanti palpiti" [21] rivals "Una voce poco fa" for distinction as the nineteenth century's most frequently embellished aria. It survives in numerous vocal versions, not to mention instrumental arrangements of all varieties. Four different embellished versions are included here.

La Cenerentola (Rome, 1817) was nearly as popular as *Il barbiere*. It was repeatedly revived in Paris after its first performance there in 1822, and it remained popular throughout Europe during the entire century. Cinderella's final aria of forgiveness and reconciliation, "Nacqui all'affanno" [13], was a favorite vehicle of embellishment during the period. *La gazza ladra* (Milan, 1817), now known primarily for its overture, was first heard in Paris at the Théâtre-Italien in 1821 and is represented here by Ninetta's exultant cavatina from act 1, "Di piacer mi balza il cor" [14]. *Mosè in Egitto* (Naples, 1818), although of great importance in Rossini's 1827 French revision (it was presented 187 times by 1865), is virtually forgotten today. It is represented by the anthology's only duet for male voices, "Parlar, spiegar" [17] for Faraone and Osiride. Rossini's *Otello* (Naples, 1816) was first heard in Paris in 1821 and occasionally revived there until Verdi's setting obscured it after 1887. Desdemona's plaintive romanza, " 'Assisa a piè' " [18], is a setting of Shakespeare's "Willow Song." *Semiramide* (Venice, 1823) was Rossini's last opera before his move to Paris, where it was first performed in 1825, the year after his arrival. The present anthology contains Arsace's cavatina "Ah, quel giorno ognor rammento" [19].

Of Rossini's five Paris operas (actually two new operas and three revisions of previous works), two are represented in this collection. *Le siège de Corinthe* (Opéra, 1826) was a revision of his *Maometto II* (Naples, 1820), and it received more than one hundred performances at the Opéra by 1844. Although it is more frequently sung in Italian, I have included Pamira's introspective aria, "Du séjour de la lumière" [20], in its original French version. Rossini's last and most originally "French" opera, *Guillaume Tell* (Opéra, 1829), was also his most successful (aside from *Il barbiere*), having received some 1,000 performances in Paris by the turn of the century. It is represented in this anthology by Mathilde's romance, "Sombre forêt" [15].

Vincenzo Bellini moved to Paris in 1833 but was able to complete only one opera (*I puritani*, Théâtre-Italien, 1835) before his early death the year of its premiere. His music had been heard there ever since 1827, even though *Beatrice di Tenda* (Venice, 1833) was not performed in Paris until 1841. Beatrice's cavatina "Ma la sola" [1] was well enough regarded to occupy a favored position in the repertoire of Jenny Lind a generation after its composition. Lind also sang Amina's aria "Ah! non credea" [2] from Bellini's *La sonnambula* (Milan, 1831—performed in Paris the same year), and Laure Cinti-Damoreau held an especial regard for the same character's cavatina "Come per me sereno" [3]. This last example is especially interesting because of its embellishment of recitative.

The music of Giacomo Meyerbeer is problematic today. Since his works have all but disappeared from the operatic repertory, I am hard-pressed to give them the space their contemporary reputation demands. German by birth and training, Italian by early stylistic influence, and French in terms of international influence, Meyerbeer was first heard in Paris in 1825. Although he never took up permanent residence, he came to spend more and more time there, setting out to acquire a thorough knowledge of French history, language, and theater in order to capitalize upon what he perceived as the French need for a national style of lyric theater. His first effort in that direction, *Robert le diable* (Opéra, 1831—here represented by Isabelle's air "En vain j'espère" [7]), not only succeeded in accomplishing his aim—it received over 100 performances by 1834 and over 700 by the end of the century—but is also credited with establishing a firm financial footing for the Opéra itself.

Native French opera composers had to compete with the Italian imports, especially before the emergence of grand opera in the 1830s. As a result, in order to assure success, French composers tended to combine the most popular elements of Italian style with what they saw as the canon of French dramatic taste. One of the most successful was François-Adrien Boieldieu (1775–1834), often known as "the French Mozart." Boieldieu is represented here by arias from two *opéras comiques*, one from the beginning of his career and the other from just after the onset of Rossini's influence. *Le calife de Bagdad* (Salle Favart, 1800) enjoyed a secure place in the repertory until 1836 and played in most major European and North American houses within a decade of its premiere. Transparent in both plot and musical texture, Késie's air "De tous les pays" [4] is an exercise in stylistic plurality that portrays the musical attractions of different European cultures under the guise of demonstrating the heroine's ability to be all things to her husband. *La dame blanche* (Opéra-Comique, 1825) is considered Boieldieu's best work and is credited with upholding "the national French comic opera almost singlehanded . . . against the blandishments of the Italian opera of Rossini."[4] Enjoying more than a thousand performances within forty years, it was influential in steering the *opéra comique* toward serious dramatic substance. Anna's air "Comme aux jours" [5] evokes the conflicting emotions of homecoming and the memory of a lost love.

Boieldieu's chief rival, Nicolas Isouard (1775–1818), enjoyed considerable Parisian success as a composer of *opéras comiques* from 1800 on, composing thirty works in that period. *Le billet de loterie* (Opéra-Comique, 1811) is a one-act comedy that remained in the repertory until 1833. Adèle's rondo "Non, je ne veux pas chanter" [6] operates on the conceit of demonstrating musically what it rejects verbally.

Finally, two examples from Mozart are included for special reasons. Although eighteenth-century opera was generally of little interest to early nineteenth-century audiences, certain works escaped this indifference. *Le nozze di Figaro*, premiered in Vienna in 1786, reached Paris by 1793, although initially without success. After a revival at the Théâtre-Italien in 1807, *Figaro* gradually gained a permanent position in the repertories of several French theaters, to the point that its music became a standard item among both French and Italian singers. Its representation in two of the embellishment sources for the present anthology demonstrates that our inclination to consider certain composers sacrosanct and "off limits" to vocal embellishment was not shared by singers of the period. Neither of the Mozart examples is the extended virtuosic vehicle we tend to judge appropriate for vocal decoration: both the duettino "Che soave zeffiretto" [8] and the arietta "Voi che sapete" [9] are deliberately simple compositions containing a certain amount of textual and musical naiveté. Accordingly, embellishment in these cases serves a different purpose: it does not demonstrate the virtuosic limits of the singer's technique but rather the singer's ability to invent tasteful ornamentation within the aesthetic limits of the original composition.

The Singers

A great part of Rossini's impact was melodic: the public, then as now, was immediately struck by the impression that his melodies were the best possible rendering of the dramatic text and its emotion. But this impact did not depend solely on composition per se—nor did contemporary audiences expect that it should—but to a nearly equal degree on the style of vocal delivery. This style, in turn, was molded by Rossini's particularly close relationship with his singers, a relationship in which he encouraged their improvisatory skills rather than, as legend still has it, opposing them. Donald Grout's statement that from 1815 Rossini "sought to curb the abuse of ornamentation by writing out the ornaments and cadenzas instead of leaving them to be improvised by singers. . . ."[5] can be read to infer that Rossini was opposed to melodic embellishment. Yet, in each case of a performer who worked closely with Rossini, the evidence shows that the composer encouraged and supported the addition of virtuosic embellishment, guiding and directing it by advice, much of it in the form of embellished versions of arias especially written out for the singer.

The case of Mme Cinti-Damoreau (née Laure Cinthie Montalant) is a particularly telling one.[6] Born in Paris in 1801, Cinti-Damoreau received her vocal training exclusively in that city; she thus had to learn the Italianate art of vocal improvisation by assiduous study. She became famous for her abilities in this art and was more than once referred to in the press (even in Paris) as an Italian singer, so completely did her vocal style justify her Italianate stage name. Her exposure to Italian vocalism preceded Rossini's arrival by nearly a decade, for she was taken on as a young girl by Angelica Catalani, then directress of the Théâtre-Italien, in 1815. Having succeeded in the Italian style in the company of Italians, she was chosen by Rossini to sing the female leads in all his Paris operas, largely because she could perform his melodies in the manner he approved. On the basis of Cinti-Damoreau's vast repertory of embellished arias, this manner must have included extemporized decoration as an essential part of melodic delivery and structure. Her success at creating roles for Auber and Adam indicates that her artistry and technique were not of value to Italian composers alone. Over half of the examples in the present collection are drawn from her volumes of embellishments, and their style will be examined below.

Giuditta Pasta (1797–1865) presents another case of a singer valued by composers not for vocal quality alone but also for her ability to embellish their melodies. She was well known for her performances of Rossini's *Otello* and *Tancredi* even before meeting the composer, and after performing *Semiramide* under his direction in London in 1824, she performed these three works as her special vehicles all over Europe, often under Rossini's direction. She worked extensively with Cinti-Damoreau in Paris, the two of them trading roles throughout the 1820s and both appearing in the 1825 premiere of *Il viaggio a Reims*. Cinti-Damoreau's admiration for Pasta seems genuine: one of Pasta's embellishments of "Di tanti palpiti" [21] is a manuscript in Cinti-Damoreau's hand labelled "*Tancredi*. Points d'Orgue et traits de Mme Pasta dans l'air de Tancredi qu'elle chantait *inimitablement!*" The present collection also contains two examples of embellishment for her in Rossini's hand [13] and [22], as well as another [21] that, though unattributed, may reflect her performance. The examples by Rossini are particularly revealing, since they show us not only what he wanted in the way of embellishment but also what he knew Pasta could do well. Even though this collection contains no examples of Pasta's ornamentation of Bellini, it cannot go unmentioned that the roles of Norma, Beatrice, and Amina were written for her, and that Bellini's distinctive style of vocal melody was much influenced by her improvisatory abilities.

The Italian tenor Giovanni Battista Rubini (1794–1854) came to Paris in 1825 and sang under Rossini's direction in *La Cenerentola* and *Otello* that year. He had a closer relationship, however, with Bellini, who wrote the leading tenor roles in *Il pirata* (1827), *La sonnambula* (1831), and *I puritani* (1835) in close consultation with him. An example of his vocal style has been drawn from Rossini's *Mosè in Egitto* [17], a duet (with the Italian baritone Antonio Tamburini) with embellishments apparently transcribed by Castil-Blaze. Antonio Tamburini (1800–1876) came to Paris in 1832 and performed a great deal of the Rossini repertory there during that decade. Like Rubini, he worked closely with Bellini, preparing the roles of Ernesto in *Il pirata* and Forth in *I puritani* in collaboration with the composer.

Jenny Lind (1820–87) is of a later generation than the singers above. Though she never worked personally with Rossini or Bellini, she was recognized as a major interpreter of both composers (especially the latter) and continued the tradition of the singer as embellisher, perhaps as a result of her early study (1841–42) with Manuel Garcia, whose style of embellishment is incorporated in the few embellishments of hers which were written down. Her relatively brief stage career was based mainly on four works: Meyerbeer's *Robert le diable*, Donizetti's *La fille du régiment*, and Bellini's *Norma* and *La sonnambula*. Of the three Lind examples included in the anthology, one is from the last-named opera [2], while the two others are from works for which she is not so well known: Bellini's *Beatrice di Tenda* [1] and Rossini's *Il barbiere di Siviglia* [12]. In two of these ([2] and [12]) she writes out her version of the entire aria with verbal directions to the singer rather than merely notating passages of embellishment.

Barbara Marchisio (1833–1919), together with her sister Carlotta (1835–72), made a remarkable career singing paired roles in the repertory of Rossini from 1858 until Carlotta's death, after which Barbara performed alone until her retirement in 1876. They came to Paris in 1860 and worked closely with Rossini in performances of *Semiramide* (in which they sang Semiramis and Arsace) and *Guillaume Tell* (in the roles of Mathilde and Jemmy). In 1864 the composer chose them to sing the first performance of his *Petite messe solennelle* and referred to them as his "incomparable interpreters." The examples included here—[3], [10], and [12]—are taken from Barbara's 1900 manuscript collection of aria embellishments.

Manuel Garcia (1805–1906) was the most famous vocal pedagogue of the nineteenth century, teaching scores of famous singers, among them his sisters Pauline Viardot-Garcia and Maria Malibran, in the course of his extraordinarily long career. His treatises reflect a concern that a style of vocal interpretation was being obscured and might be in danger of dying out entirely if he did not make careful record of all its precepts and techniques. Thus, his writings give the student much more by way of vocal direction (including breath, tone, rubato, tempo, and dramatic interpretation) than do those of other pedagogues. In addition, Garcia provided samples of embellishment style, often attributing them to certain singers in the context of specific arias. Frustrating for the purposes of this anthology is the fact that Garcia seldom wrote out an interpretation of an entire aria but rather presented interpretations of individual phrases. One example is seen in [10]: Garcia offers half a dozen different choices for the embellishment of a passage only three measures in length. One of the few cases in which he set forth his recommendations for a complete composition is found in [11].

Josefa Gassier (1821–66) was a Spanish soprano whose repertory centered on the works of Rossini, Bellini, and Donizetti. Little is known about her career, and the embellishments attributed to her by Castil-Blaze for "Una voce poco fa" [12] are included in this anthology for the purpose of comparison with those of the more famous singers who sang this most celebrated of cavatinas. Unless Castil-Blaze was mistaken in his transcription, the notation of Gassier's embellishments in G major (one step higher than the usual soprano key) indicates what must have been an astonishing upper range.

Mme Gregoire is known to us only from Rossini's dedication of his autograph embellishments for "Di tanti palpiti" ([21] in this edition). Presumably she was an amateur singer friendly with the composer.

The Music

What do we learn from these embellishments concerning how performers and pedagogues thought about vocal music and its performance? It is apparent that they conceived of embellishment as bound by certain rules, which we can perceive by examining how certain types of embellishments are managed in musical context.

The cadenza is the best-known type of embellishment and the one easiest to understand in terms of musical structure. It is normally placed on the chord preceding a dominant-tonic cadence and is assumed to bring the musical motion to a halt while the singer engages in a free display of improvisatory abilities. This display typically begins with a sustained high pitch, either taken immediately or approached from below, then continues with passagework featuring scales, arpeggios, and/or appoggiaturas, which allow the voice to descend from its initial height in an affecting manner and to arrive at a pause for breath. A short cadenza may conclude at this point (see Cinti-Damoreau's five options for [15], m. 76). A longer one may go forward to investigate related tonal regions through the sequential use of short motives (see Lind's cadenza at m. 37 of [1]). The cadenza winds down by descending in pitch and abating in virtuosity until it joins the cadential pattern written by the composer, thus signaling the resumption of musical motion.

The placement of the cadenza within the larger musical form offers wider choices to the singer than usually imagined; its location in the final measures of an aria is not the only (nor even the most frequent) one. Most cavatinas do not have cadenzas at the end but rather at interior points of arrival (see [12a] and [12b], m. 41, and [21], m. 63). Arias that are slower may have them not only at the final cadence but also at any other focal point along the way. In Bellini's "Ah! non credea mirarti" [2], Jenny Lind sang a cadenza in the final measures of the vocal line (m. 39) and also at m. 30, which is not the end of anything but rather the point where the secondary tonal focus of the aria is clearly established.

It is apparent that cadenzas function within the formal design of the composition to mark points of musical arrival. It is not apparent that they have any relationship to text expression or portrayal of character: no example in this collection shows a cadenza placed in a musical context that serves these latter considerations at the expense of the former. However, a second type of embellishment—that of a repeated motive—seems to serve both criteria. This type can be distinguished from the cadenza in that it lies within the ongoing fabric of a melodic line and thus does not interrupt musical motion. Its governing policy would seem to be that stated by Garcia—"One must vary a thought each time it is repeated"[7]—and its ethos, that of providing cumulative impact to the repetitions of motives as well as to their repetitions of text. Bellini's "Come per me sereno" [3] provides an example: from m. 76 (the beginning of the cabaletta) to its end, the aria builds in intensity through the recurrence of short melodic motives. The progressive virtuosity found in such extensive embellishments allows us to presume that a singer would sing the first appearance of a motive as written and then begin an ever-increasing display of ornamentation thereafter, with the result that the last statements become overpowering. It is interesting to compare Cinti-Damoreau's mm. 83 with 102, 85 with 104, 87 with 106, and then to look at Barbara Marchisio's mm. 140–48 for a comparison of treatment of the same motives. The effect is not merely one of increasing complexity of embellishment but also of increasing intensity of dramatic statement, corresponding admirably to the demands of the characterization, which call here for the expression of near-collapse from excitement.

A third type of embellishment serves another function and seems to obey different rules in terms of placement and characterization. It is hard to label this type concisely because it does not occur at set places in the musical form, nor is it applied to specific types of phrasing. I refer to situations in which singers use their vocal ability to fulfil what they see as a composer's unrealized intent. This may take the form of substituting higher pitches, adding more rapid motion, inserting wider leaps, and the like. In such cases, the singer is not necessarily imposing his or her own concerns on the composer's design but rather discerning where the composer's ideas may be in need of fleshing out. Examples are seen in Cinti-Damoreau's treatment of "Du séjour de la lumière" [20]. At m. 20 she takes the figure written by Rossini and (without expanding range or virtuosity) enhances the composer's use of an upward-resolving appoggiatura by adding another one. In mm. 27–28 she expands upon the sequential figure by changing its direction and rhythm, then adds an extra turn to the appoggiatura figures in order to bring the phrase to a close. Then in m. 29 she realizes the expressive potential of Rossini's melody not by adding embellishment but by removing it, simplifying the line to render the sighing "hélas" and to throw into stronger relief her elaborated passages at mm. 30–31, which once again feature the upward-resolving appoggiatura. Pasta's version of "Nacqui all'affanno" ([13], mm. 55ff.) abounds in such simplifications of the composer's vocal line for the purposes of characterization, as well as to accommodate a voice whose effective range was somewhat higher.

Although singers habitually warned that embellishment must conform to the requirements of the text, it is evident that they referred to its meaning rather than its declamation: it is difficult to find examples in which embellishment underscores syllable length or poetic accentuation at the expense of other considerations. Garcia says that "the meaning of the words determines . . . the ornaments and the style of their performance."[8] Seldom, in his choice of examples for embellishment and commentary, does he heed the accentual characteristics of the text, while regularly providing embellishments for weak or unimportant syllables. Cinti-Damoreau dutifully fulfils the expectation of her native culture by warning her students, "We French do not permit ourselves to breathe in the middle of a word, to repeat a syllable, . . . in sum, we must not sacrifice the words for the notes but, quite the contrary, sacrifice the notes for the words."[9] Yet her examples regularly ignore her own warning for the sake of vocalism or characterization.

The most telling evidence of how singers thought (or were supposed to think) about text and embellishment is that provided by Rossini himself. The examples he wrote for specific singers reveal some surprises, especially concerning treatment of text in recitatives. In his version of the recitative to "Di tanti palpiti" [21] for Mme Gregoire, Rossini begins conventionally enough, writing out appoggiaturas and adding simple turns. Yet note the divergent rhythm, the dynamic contrast spelled out for "dolce, ingrata," and the *animato* interposed at m. 28. And when he arrives at "comincia il core a respirar," he writes out three measures of passagework that would not be out of place at the medial cadence of a cavatina. As the recitative continues, Rossini becomes increasingly expressive in his embellishment, adding floridity even to noncadential phrases, at mm. 40 and 50. If it is borne in mind that Mme Gregoire was most probably a nonprofessional singer, the emphasis at the recitative's final cadence (mm. 63–64) on expressivity will only seem appropriate, by contrast with the more demanding fioriture sung by Pasta and Cinti-Damoreau. (Note, though, the similarity of approach to the fifth degree before the final tonic.) Rossini's own embellishment of the recitative "Lasciami: non t'ascolto"[22] for Pasta, the skilled professional, bears out the conclusion that he considered such vocalism essential to the declaiming of musical speech.

One significant aspect of the practice of embellishment revealed by the sources of this anthology is that singers normally added their most virtuosic displays to passages already quite florid, leaving the simpler, more cantabile passages unadorned. Today's singer often assumes that, when a composer has written in a virtuosic style, he has set a limit of sorts as concerns vocal display; but the singers in this anthology evidently viewed such florid writing as an invitation to add their own skills to those of the composer. Again, we do well to look to Rossini himself and to what he considered appropriate. Comparing the cavatina of "Di tanti palpiti" [21] with the composer's embellished version, we see that Rossini's original score does not represent the limit of his expectations of virtuosity. At m. 100 he asks Mme Gregoire to add considerable decoration to the *conduit* he has written to reintroduce the main motive. In the further course of the piece, Rossini does not hesitate to enhance the technical demands of his own music, including the embellishment of already virtuosic passages. Rounding off the main theme (before the stretta), he specifies a dotted ascent in m. 118, then an octave leap and florid descent in m. 119 (a turn that Cinti-Damoreau may also have learned from him, to judge from her treatment of m. 119). At m. 126 he asks for an octave leap and scalar descent between phrases—closing up what was a rest in the original melody and setting a high point (*forte*) before the sudden *pianissimo* with which he ushers in the final phase of the stretta. From this point on, Rossini not only has the singer embellishing above and below his original melody but also intensifies the dynamic range (cf. the *fortissimo* at mm. 132 and 138 and the syncopated accents in m. 134 with the "unadorned" vocal part). Such freedom of treatment, involving simplification as well as complication of the melody, indicates that singers were accustomed to amplify the expressive character of a composition within a broad range of vocal possibilities, and to do so at the composer's behest. Embellishments written out by the composer seem not to have deterred the inventive powers of singers but rather to have challenged them.

The various sources of embellishment that form the basis of this anthology must be recognized as having differing purposes. Some are archival, others pedagogical, and within the pedagogical framework there are various methodologies at work: Garcia presents a great deal of verbal instruction together with fragmentary examples in an effort to instill principles of performance rather than give the student complete arias to memorize. Cinti-Damoreau, on the other hand, tends to provide extended examples of her own most successful embellishments to serve as models for the invention of her students:

> I do not give them to you in order that you perform them at any cost, even in spite of your constitution and your nature. They are varied formulas, which I offer so that, later, your taste will lead you, within the limit of your ability, to invent others that suit you properly.[10]

Barbara Marchisio admits to no pedagogical purpose whatever. She claims her collection to be purely a memento of a bygone style:

> Good friend,
>
> I offer these dear remembrances of my happy career to you, who have been able to gather once more the last sighs, the sparks that remain of our beautiful Italian song. And I offer them neither for their own merit nor with the remotest hope that one day they would become useful to the young students of your conservatory.
>
> No, my friend, with every passing day I become more convinced that at present those who aspire to my beloved art are all following quite a different path with too much haste and too little enthusiasm! I am giving them to you only because I am sure that you will jealously guard these little compositions that remind you of the vocal partnership of the fortunate sisters.[11]

Jenny Lind's embellishments were assembled and published by other hands and have, like Marchisio's manuscript, an archival purpose. It is essential to note that none of the collections intended that a singer memorize and perform examples verbatim; even Cinti-Damoreau assumes that her students will work out their own embellishments using hers as models. It is by using this collection in this spirit that the memory of these singers will best be served.

Sources

The components of this edition are based on several different kinds of sources: orchestral scores, piano-vocal scores, and embellishments both in print and in manuscripts of variable neatness and completeness. Each kind of source has required a different approach, as set forth under Editorial Methods below. Although a great deal of careful attention has gone into the preparation of all aspects of the anthology, only the embellishments themselves claim to be critically edited. I cannot attempt to stand in judgment concerning the authority of the orchestral scores from which I have worked, for that is the task of editors of ongoing opera omnia, nor can I claim to have arrived at critically acceptable versions of works that have stymied the best editorial efforts of interested scholars. The main purpose of this edition is to present authentic examples of vocal embellishment, and thus all else, even the piano-vocal scores themselves, is context, even if indispensable context.

Piano-Vocal Scores

The piano-vocal scores contained in this anthology are meant to be arrangements serviceable to performers, and to that end they are based upon the most reliable source available for each aria—be it a modern critical edition, a modern facsimile reproduction of the composer's autograph orchestral score, the earliest available orchestral score published by a house known to have had a working relationship with the composer, or, failing all these, the earliest available piano-vocal score published by such a house. These sources are indicated at the head of the Critical Notes for each aria, although their readings are not usually reported in cases of emendation. Further specifics of this policy are given in Editorial Methods.

Texts

It has been necessary to adopt a similarly informal approach to the presentation of the verbal texts of the arias since, as Philip Gossett has convincingly demonstrated in his critical study of Rossini's scores and libretti, neither composers nor publishers seem to have paid much attention to the presentation of libretto texts as literature, with predictable results for consistency of spelling, line division, punctuation, etc.[12] The kinds of text sources consulted for this anthology are described under Editorial Methods, and individual sources are identified in the Critical Notes and (as necessary) in Texts and Translations.

Embellishments

The embellishments themselves stem from at least nine different singers, as recorded in the following sources.

CINTI-DAMOREAU

Laure Cinti-Damoreau. *Méthode de chant composée pour ses classes du Conservatoire par Mme Cinti-Damoreau*. Paris: Au Ménestrel, 1849. 60 leaves, 25.5 x 33 cm (hereafter Cinti-Damoreau, *Méthode*).

———. "Points d'orgue et variantes composées par Mme Cinti-Damoreau pour differents Airs." Undated MS. 57 leaves, 14.6 x 22.2 cm (hereafter Cinti-Damoreau I).

———. Untitled MS (n.d.). 36 leaves, 14.6 x 19 cm (hereafter Cinti-Damoreau II).

———. Untitled MS (n.d.). 28 leaves, 15.2 x 23 cm (hereafter Cinti-Damoreau III).

———. Untitled MS (n.d.). 32 leaves, 14.6 x 24 cm (hereafter Cinti-Damoreau VI).

The Cinti-Damoreau collection at Lilly Library, Indiana University, includes the printed *Méthode de chant* and seven manuscript notebooks. The notebooks range from a formal anthology (notebook I), in a hand so fine that it looks engraved, to informal (sometimes barely decipherable) sketchbooks (e.g., notebook III). (See plates 1–3.) Cinti-Damoreau II seems to have been started as an anthology (like notebook I) and to have been turned into a sketchbook. For the present edition, the most significant of the sources are the print and the first three notebooks. (Notebook VI is included in the above list because it gives better readings of the embellishments for [9].) Together, the eight books contain (among other things) some 200 passages of embellishment for the arias in Cinti-Damoreau's repertoire, of which over 100 can be deciphered and applied to specific arias.[13] They include cadenzas as well as embellishments for passages within the ongoing fabric of arias, and these in turn illustrate the technique of this Parisian soprano for whom Rossini wrote the leading roles in his Paris operas. In addition to Bellini and Rossini, virtually every French opera composer of the second quarter of the nineteenth century is represented in her repertoire. The collection was purchased by the Lilly Library from Everett Helm in 1971.

MARCHISIO

Barbara Marchisio. "Cadenze e variante composte e eseguite dalle sorelle Marchisio." MS in 2 vols. (vol. 1: 12 leaves containing 90 examples; vol. 2: 16 leaves containing 54 examples, both 32.5 x 24 cm). Naples, 1900. Cary Collection 142, Pierpont Morgan Library, New York.

This collection represents the repertoire of Barbara Marchisio and her sister Carlotta, whose careers followed Cinti-Damoreau's by one generation. Since the Marchisios performed together a great deal, these volumes include many embellishments of duets. They contain a smaller proportion of inner variants than those of Cinti-Damoreau, concentrating instead upon cadenzas of the full-stop type for Italian operas. The only French works included are those of Rossini and Meyerbeer. Of the handful of examples that Luigi Ricci attributes to either "Marchisio" or "the Marchisio sisters," all but three are taken from the second of the two manuscript volumes. None of Ricci's examples are duplicated in the present anthology.[14]

GARCIA

Manuel Garcia. *Ecole de Garcia: Traité complet de l'art du chant* . . . 2 vols. Mayence. Les fils de B. Schott, 1847.

———. *Hints on Singing*. Translated from the French by Beata Garcia. London: B. Ascherberg & Co., 1894.

Garcia's *Traité* is a summa of nineteenth-century vocal interpretation and thus an important source for examples of aria embellishment. In the third chapter ("Changements") of part 2, Garcia not only explains the stereotypic ornaments—appoggiatura, trill, and mordent—but also provides models for the free embellishment of passages in specific arias. Many of these embellishments are unattributed and may be presumed to be Garcia's own. Others are identified as transcriptions from the performances of famous contemporary singers —Garcia's father, Pasta, Cinti-Damoreau, Tamburini, Sontag, and Tacchinardi-Persiani, among others. The materials appended after the fifth chapter are also noteworthy in this connection. They provide models for cadential diminution—that is, embellishment not intended to break the motion of the aria; models for cadenzas of the full-stop type; and the "interpretive analyses" for which Garcia is justly famous. The present edition includes examples of all of these types. *Hints on Singing* is a shorter volume (77 pages) written in dialogue form. While it lacks appendixes of embellishment models, it does contain short examples of embellishment scattered throughout its pages.

LIND

Henry Scott Holland and W[illiam] S. Rockstro. *Memoir of Madame Jenny Lind-Goldschmidt: Her Early Art-Life and Dramatic Career*. 2 vols. London: John Murray; New York: Charles Scribner and Sons, 1891.

Holland and Rockstro's memoir of Jenny Lind's early career is based on materials collected by her husband, Otto Goldschmidt. An appendix to volume 2 includes seven embellishments of arias in her repertoire. These embellishments have been cited, and parts of two of them included, in the fifth edition of *Grove's Dictionary of Music and Musicians*, s.v. "singing." The transcriptions in the present edition are complete, more accurate, and have the advantage of showing the embellishments in the context of the aria. A particular distinction of the Lind examples is that, unlike most other sources, they give the vocal line in full so that one is never in doubt where the embellishments should be placed.

GASSIER, RUBINI, AND TAMBURINI

Castil-Blaze [François Henri Joseph Blaze]. *Théâtres lyriques de Paris: Recueil de musique (de 1100 à 1855)*. Paris: Castil-Blaze, pl. no. C.B. 86 [1855].

The *Recueil de musique* is the volume of music examples that accompanied Castil-Blaze's pioneering history of the lyric theater in Paris. Most of its four hundred pages are devoted to representative selections from French and Italian opera of the seventeenth and eighteenth centuries. However, tucked in among these scores are four pages of "Traits de chanteurs célèbres," twenty-three embellished passages of varying lengths attributed to singers mostly contemporary with Castil-Blaze—Malibran, Gassier, Tamburini, Rubini, Catalani, and Marchesi, inter alia. There are also a few representatives of the art of eighteenth-century singers (among them Farinelli). At the end of the fourth page is a chart showing the vocal ranges of twenty-five French and Italian singers, among them Catalani, Malibran, Rubini, Nourrit, Tamburini, and Levasseur.

PASTA AND GREGOIRE

Rossini autograph, in folder entitled "Cadenze per Giuditta Pasta." 3 pages, 22 x 28.5 cm. Cary Collection 170, Pierpont Morgan Library, New York. Embellishments for *Tancredi*, "Lasciami non t'ascolto" [22].

Rossini autograph, in folder entitled "Cadenze per Giuditta Pasta." 3 pages, 22.5 x 31.5 cm. Cary Collection 171, Pierpont Morgan Library, New York. Embellishments for *La Cenerentola*, "Nacqui all'affanno" [13].

Rossini autograph, signed "Quelques ornements sur l'air de Tancredi pour l'usage de Mad^{me} Gregoire par son ami G.

Rossini. Passy ce 15 Août 1858." 3 pages, 27 x 34.5 cm. Cary Collection 177, Pierpont Morgan Library, New York. Embellishments for *Tancredi*, "Di tanti palpiti" [21] (see plate 4).

Rossini is known to have accommodated numerous singers by writing out appropriate embellishments for them at their request, and these three examples are part of that sizable literature. Philip Gossett has appended the embellishments for Gregoire [21] and for Pasta [22] to his critical edition of *Tancredi*.[15] Though the embellishments are not presented in the context of the original arias, their placement is indicated by means of measure numbers. Gossett dates the Pasta embellishments for [22] circa 1820 (when Pasta was singing *Tancredi* in Paris) on the basis of Rossini's use of the soprano clef, as opposed to his later adoption of the G clef as in the 1858 ornaments for Mme Gregoire.

Anonymous

"Oh Patria! dolce e ingrata Patria, recit. e | Tu che accendi questo core, | CAVATINA, | In the Opera of | Il Tancredi. | Composed by | Rossini | Arranged with an Accompaniment | for the | Piano | Forte." London: Clementi and Co. No. 26 Cheapside, n.d. [1821–28].

This early nineteenth-century print of "O patria" from Rossini's *Tancredi* exemplifies a popular publishing convention, that of issuing an aria in an embellished version, often "as sung by" a famous singer (see plate 5). Though this example (hereafter cited as Anonymous) does not bear the name of a singer, its publication followed the London premiere of *Tancredi* and may have attended Rossini's visit to the city in 1823–24.[16] Since Giuditta Pasta was featured in the title role in the 1824 London performance of *Tancredi*, it is possible that this source represents her embellishments, as do two of the three Rossini autographs above.

Editorial Methods

As a general principle, this edition presents embellishments within the context of entire arias. Recitative is included as well when it, too, is subject to embellishment or when its exclusion would be inappropriate (see [3], [4], [16], [18], and [21]). In exceptional cases, space constraints have necessitated departures from this general principle. The fast movement of "Ecco ridente in cielo" [11] is omitted here, since the embellishment source in question, Garcia's *Traité*, focuses exclusively on the slow movement. To have reprinted the cabaletta here would have brought little significant improvement over the countless prints of this music readily available. A similar consideration prompted the omission of mm. 130–220 of the duet "Lasciami: non t'ascolto" [21]. Choral parts, too, are omitted from this edition, but their presence is reported in the Critical Notes.

Arias

The arias are presented in piano-vocal scores, prepared by the editor with reference to sources identified in the Critical Notes for each item, although variants in those sources are not reported. Unless otherwise noted, these sources are orchestral scores. In some cases, it was possible to consult a modern scholarly edition (for arias [8]–[12], [14], [16], [21], and [22]). Otherwise, I have turned to modern facsimile reproductions, either of the composer's manuscript (for arias [13], [17], [18], and [19]) or of a published contemporaneous score whose relation to the composer's intentions has been ascertained through modern scholarship (arias [1], [7], [15], and [20]). In one case ([5]), I have consulted a later print (the earliest score available to me) issued by a publisher known to have had a working relationship with the composer. Failing all of the above, I have resorted to contemporaneous piano-vocal scores (arias [2]–[4] and [6]), again choosing the earliest available score, preferably one issued by a house known to have had a working relationship with the composer.

The vocal melody of each piano-vocal score in this edition adheres (with regard to pitch, rhythm, and expression marks) to that found in the respective sources. Musically significant exceptions are reported in the Critical Notes. The piano accompaniments make no scholarly pretensions but are designed as practical reductions with which pianists can work. In all cases, I have been guided by the models of the earliest piano-vocal scores available to me (likewise reported in the Critical Notes for each item), though most of these arrangements have been revised upon consultation of the orchestral sources described above. Idiomatic articulations specified for orchestral instruments are only approximated in the piano reductions. Beaming in these reductions has been tacitly regularized in accordance with modern convention.

Texts

The texts of these arias present particular problems to the editor, especially those of determining authority of spelling, punctuation, capitalization, and line division. Editions of libretti (both contemporaneous and modern) are often not much help. In this edition, whenever a piano-vocal score is based on a modern critical edition (i.e., arias [8]–[21], [14], [16], [21], and [22]), I have also relied upon it for an authoritative version of the poetic text. Otherwise, I have taken the texts presented in the respective aria sources as the basis for this edition, supplementing these as needed by reference to other sources for guidance in the regularization of spelling, punctuation, and line division. (These other sources are cited individually in the Texts and Translations.[17]) No separate attempt has been made to establish critical authority for these texts; like the piano accompaniments, they are intended to be serviceable rather than scholarly.

The various sources of the arias and embellishments in this edition present the texts in several languages. For the "unembellished" vocal melodies, I have adopted the language used in the principal source for each arrangement (which is not necessarily the language of the embellishment texts) and for the presentation of the text in the Texts and Translations. The English translations have been prepared by the editor and are meant to be literal rather than performable.

Embellishments

The foremost editorial task concerning the embellishments is to locate properly ornaments whose position within the given aria, or even within a given opera, may not be specified by the source. This becomes problematic chiefly with the manuscript sources and particularly with the Cinti-Damoreau notebooks; it is not an issue with sources that present at least a semblance of the entire aria melody (as do Lind and the interpretative analyses in Garcia, *Traité*). In the most difficult cases, I have proceeded from the assumption that the source presents the embellishments in the order of their performance within each aria, then relied on melodic, harmonic, and verbal contexts to arrive at a fitting location for each embellishment. Whenever a given embellishment could be located at any of several repetitions of a given phrase, I have placed the embellishment at the last recurrence in order to achieve the effect of cumulative virtuosity, as recommended by Garcia in his *Traité*: "Pieces that are based on the return of a motive . . . are particularly apt to receive variations. These variations must follow an increasing progression in their placement."[18] Conversely, whenever a source gives (legible) alternate embellishments for a single phrase, these are included in the edition with their original labels (e.g., *autre*, *bis*, and *ou*). If the alternate embellishments are not decipherable (as occasionally in the Cinti-Damoreau notebooks), their presence is reported in the Critical Notes. In several sources the individual embellishments are numbered (see plate 2, for example). These numerals have been tacitly suppressed in this anthology, though their presence is mentioned in the Critical Notes.

A number of sources present embellishments in keys different from those of the aria sources. (See the embellishments for arias [1], [2], [12], and [21].) While these keys do reflect the range and technique of the respective singers, the limits of space in this edition have made transposition of the given embellishment seem the preferable alternative to printing the arias in several transpositions. In such cases, the original key of the embellishment is indicated in the Critical Notes. The sole exception to this policy is made for Rossini's "Una voce poco fa" [12], which has traditionally been performed in either of the two keys presented here: the original key of E [12a], matching the embellishments of Cinti-Damoreau and Marchisio; and the key of F [12b], matching Lind's transcription (given here in full). The short embellishment in G by Gassier has been transposed down to match the second version. Apart from these cases of transposition, Rossini's autograph embellishments for Pasta have been transcribed from soprano clef to G-clef in this edition.

Every attempt has been made to preserve the singers' intentions as expressed in the notation of the embellishment sources. The edition reproduces the rhythmic groupings (i.e., the patterns of beams and flags) of each source, and stem direction is but sparingly accommodated to modern convention. When the rhythms of the source seem irrational, I have tried to suggest their proper performance through vertical alignment with the original vocal melody without altering the rhythms, since their very "incorrectness" may suggest the liberties a singer expected to take (or remembered having taken) in a given passage. Whenever emendation of pitch or rhythm has been unavoidable, I have reported the reading of the embellishment source in the Critical Notes. Where evident omissions have been supplied, they appear in square brackets. Barlines supplied by the editor appear as dashed lines.

The embellishment sources do not always reflect the modern convention that the force of an accidental carries to the end of the measure unless cancelled by another accidental. This is especially noticeable in cadenzas of the full-stop type, where the measure itself is temporarily broken: accidentals are repeated where modern convention would not require them, while cancelling accidentals are often not provided where modern convention would require them. In general, I have not deleted any redundant accidental that seemed useful for performers. (Any deletions are reported in the Critical Notes.) Editorial cancelling accidentals have been added, in square brackets, in any instance where the intended inflection might be ambiguous. (Any cautionary accidentals, likewise supplied by the editor, appear in parentheses.) However, where the original notation, in its given musical context, is unambiguous, editorial cancelling accidentals have not been added to the embellishment, even though they would, strictly speaking, be required by modern convention.

In cadenzas of the full-stop type, it often happens that the embellishment staff (or staves) may have many more notes than the original vocal staff. When appropriate, the notation on the original staff is graphically stretched to accommodate the more numerous notes of the embellishment, not to imply anything about the performance of the original melody but to clarify melodic relationships for the comparison of embellishment with original. In like manner, the vertical alignment among different embellished versions of the same cadence has occasionally been manipulated to clarify melodic relationships. By fostering comparative study of embellished versions, this edition may afford that grasp of underlying principles that will permit students to improvise embellishments of their own.

The articulation marks and dynamic indications of the embellishment sources are rendered as exactly as possible in this edition, though their location above or below the staff may have been tacitly regularized in accordance with modern convention. Slurs and ties provided by the editor appear as dashed curves. One kind of symbol, peculiar to Rossini autographs, deserves special comment here. This is the closed dynamic "hairpin."

According to Alberto Zedda, Rossini's use of these signs is nearly unique but also consistent and unequivocal. "This typical closed fork is an indication of force, an *accento* or *sforzato* that cleanly cuts off the crescendo or immediately begins the diminuendo. Such an interpretation, extended to the closed accent (▷), allows the assertion that it ought to be a stronger and more marked effect than the open accent."[19] Following the policy of the Rossini complete works edition, I have retained these symbols wherever they occur in the sources.

The embellishment sources indicate that singers commonly took liberties with the aria texts. As a rule, this edition reproduces all embellishment texts in their original and frequently careless state—adding only hyphens to show word division—so long as the singer's intent can be discerned and makes musical sense. Where that intent cannot be discerned, or scribal error is evident, I have followed the reading of the aria source and reported the reading of the embellishment source in the Critical Notes. In any case, the embellishment text can easily be compared and (if desired) likened with the text underlaid to the unembellished vocal line. Editorial additions to the embellishment texts are marked with square brackets; these additions are usually based on the text of the aria source.

Cinti-Damoreau's embellishments sometimes use a French text where the aria source uses Italian. (See arias [9], [14], [16], [19], and [21].) With one exception, the French text is retained in this edition, even though a version of the entire aria in that language has not been incorporated. The exception is made for "Voi che sapete" [9], which singers in this country would have little reason to perform in French. Cinti-Damoreau's text is reported in the Critical Notes for that aria. For the remaining arias, an editorial underlay of the Italian text appears beneath the French text of the source.

Finally, two of the sources make a typographical distinction (common in nineteenth-century prints) between embellishment and principal melodic notes, which this edition has sought to retain. The Clementi print of "Di tanti palpiti" [21] (described above in Sources; also see plate 5) shows principal melodic notes full-size with downward stems and ornamental notes in cue size with upward stems. Coincident notes appear full size with stems in both directions. Cinti-Damoreau I (see plate 2) uses three different sizes of notation: full size for the principal melodic pitches, a smaller size for Cinti-Damoreau's variants, and an even smaller size for ornamental figures (turns, appoggiaturas, etc.) within these variants. Only the last of these typographic distinctions has been reproduced in this edition. On occasion Cinti-Damoreau's notation of the original vocal line (as indicated by the full-size notes) differs from the version found in the aria source and may be assumed to represent her (not always reliable) recollection of the composition. Many of these divergent readings are presented on the embellishment staves of this edition as variants; where they seem to reflect an inconsequential slip of memory, they have been recorded in the Critical Notes.

Critical Notes

The Critical Notes identify the following for each embellished aria: (A) an aria source (i.e., an orchestral score used as the basis of the vocal melody and consulted for arranging the piano accompaniment) and/or (B) an accompaniment source (i.e., an early piano-vocal score serving as model for the piano accompaniment) and (C) one or more embellishment sources (i.e., the manuscripts and prints that contain the embellishments edited here). These kinds of sources are discussed above under Sources and Editorial Methods. Individual embellishment sources are cited by the names of the singers—when necessary, together with a short form of the title (e.g., Garcia, *Hints*). The Cinti-Damoreau notebooks are abbreviated to CD I, CD II, and so forth, and her *Méthode* is abbreviated to CDM. Any original inscriptions in the embellishment sources appear in quotation marks.

Following each list of sources are reports of individual variants between the sources (usually the embellishment sources) and the edition. These notes also comment on certain features of the original notation. Note counts in these reports include all ornamental notes, and the following abbreviations are used: m(m). = measure(s); emb(s) = embellishment(s). Variant text appears in italics. Pitch is identified by the familiar system, whereby c' = middle C, and so forth.

[1] *Ma la sola*

SOURCES

A. Vincenzo Bellini, *Beatrice di Tenda* (Rome: Pietro Pittarelli, [183?]; facsimile reprint with an introduction by Philip Gossett, New York: Garland, 1980).

B. Vincenzo Bellini, *Beatrice di Tenda* (Milan: Ricordi, pl. no. 45541 [after 1857]).[20]

C. Lind, appendix, 1–2.

CD II, 56–57, "Beatrice di Tenda / O miei fedeli" (eleven passages in pencil, ten numbered).

NOTES

There are chorus parts at mm. 25–36, 75–94, and 118–36. Lind presents embs in the key of E-flat; CD II, in D.

M. 23, Lind emb labelled "*Cadenza (a)*." M. 24, text *na-* two notes later in CD II. M. 25, *-tio* under note 1 in CD II. M. 29, notes 4–20 written a third higher in source A—edition follows source B; notes 10 and 11 are sixteenth-notes in CD II. M. 33, emb, "incorrectness" of note 1 may indicate that Cinti-Damoreau expected a slight lengthening of the note; rhythm of last eight notes has been emended from source pattern of eighth-note plus three sixteenth-notes. M. 34, in CD II *tal* is two notes earlier in bar and last note has natural sign, probably meant for next last note; in performing the emb in m. 34, the singer may wish to adopt the text alignment of source A if that of CD II seems awkward. M. 34, note 14, to m. 35, note 1, written a third lower in source B—edition follows source A. M. 37, Lind emb labelled "*Cadenza (b)*." M. 38, grace note is ♯' in source A, with no slur; text is *-so* in CD II. Mm. 56–57, last note of m. 56 in source A has text *-tir*, m. 57 has text *do-vu-ti a* under notes 1, 2–3, 4–5, and 6–7— edition follows underlay of parallel passage at mm. 99–100 in source A. M. 102, note 3 has text *su* in source A. M. 106, emb, rests 2–4 are sixteenth-rests in CD II. M. 114, note 1 is g#", note 14 is e" in source A—edition follows source B.

[2] *Ah! non credea mirarti*

SOURCES

B. Vincenzo Bellini, *La sonnambula*, riduzione del M° Luigi Truzzi (Milan: Gio. Ricordi; Florence: Ricordi e Comp°., pl. no. 5287–88, 1831).

C. Lind, appendix, 10–12.

NOTES

All notes refer to readings in Lind. The instruction regarding performance of the cadenzas appears on p. 12 of that source.

M. 25, notes 5 and 6 are sixteenth-notes. M. 34, note 2 has text *Pa-*.

[3] *Come per me sereno*

SOURCES

B. Vincenzo Bellini, *La sonnambula*, riduzione del M° Luigi Truzzi (Milan: Gio. Ricordi; Florence: Ricordi e Comp°., pl. no. 5287–88, 1831).

C. CD I, 38–41, "Air de la Somnambule" (twenty-one numbered passages in ink; see plate 2).

CDM, 47, "Point d'Orgue pour l'Air de la SOMNAMBULA."

Marchisio, "Sonnambula Cavatina" (four passages in ink, three of them alternates).

NOTES

CD I is a fair ink copy with occasional expression and articulation marks in pencil, which have been incorporated into the edition without further report. From m. 86 to the end of the aria, CD I is written in the key of G.

All notes refer to readings in CD I.

M. 25, notes 2 and 3 have text *spesso*; note 1 is same size as notes 2 and 3 but probably meant to be sung as an appoggiatura in place of note 2. M. 59, note 20 is an eighth-note. Mm. 161–62, CD I has a semilegible pencil sketch, consisting of four ascending half-note trills, above emb reproduced here. M. 173, CD I has a semilegible pencil sketch above embs reproduced here —sketch consists of half-note f" (g" in this transposition) followed by flourish of sixteenth-notes terminating on g' (a' in this transposition).

[4] *De tous les pays*

SOURCES

B. [François-]Adrien Boieldieu, *Le calife de Bagdad*, nouvelle réduction au piano avec les indications d'orchestre par Adrien Boieldieu (Paris: Henri Heugel, pl. no. 3295 [ca. 1885]).

C. CD I, 4–6, "Traits et Points d'Orgue du Calife de Bagdad" (thirty-one numbered passages in ink).

NOTES

M. 7, emb, note 1 is a'—stem direction of note 1 suggests that it was intended as a grace note, though note is same size as surrounding notes; emb has barline before note 5. M. 8, emb, note 6 is sharped. M. 36, emb, note 1 is quarter-note. M. 106, source B gives instruction "(elle valse)." M. 121, source B gives instruction "(elle valse encore)." M. 228, emb, notated as sixteenth-note triplets. M. 243, emb, text *nou-* under note 5.

[5] *Comme aux jours*

SOURCES

A. François-Adrien Boieldieu, *La dame blanche*, partition d'orchestre revue par Gustav Kogel (Leipzig: C. F. Peters, pl. no. 6379 [ca. 1880].

B. François-Adrien Boieldieu, *La dame blanche* (Paris: E. Girod, pl. no. E.G. 3286 [ca. 1855]).

C. CD III, 19–21, "La Dame Blanche" (seventeen numbered passages in pencil, three of them alternates; see plate 3).

NOTES

M. 43, edition follows notation of CD III, but singer may want to hold note 1 to second beat before continuing emb *ad libitum*. Mm. 45–62, missing in source A; source B marks this passage with segno at either end and provides footnote: "Les 17 mesures comprises entre les signes sont supprimées dans la grande Partition"—edition follows source B. Mm. 103–5, alternate emb is sketched on p. 20 of CD III at ends of staves 4 and 6, and first part of emb is rewritten on p. 19 more legibly but without text—edition follows clearer notation of p. 19 and underlay of p. 20. Mm. 123–32, missing in source A—edition follows source B. M. 128, emb, illegible letters above note 1 could be a *tr* sign. Mm. 136–38, emb is labelled "Bis," to be an alternative to emb placed at mm. 134–36.

[6] *Non, je ne veux pas chanter*

SOURCES

B. Nicolas Isouard, *Le billet de loterie*, partition piano et chant (Paris: Brandus, pl. no. B. et Cie 9398 [ca. 1846]).

C. CD I, 1–3, "Points d'Orgue et Variantes de l'Air du Billet de loterie" (twenty-six numbered passages in ink).

CDM, 105–6, "Le Billet de Loterie" and "Rentrée dans la même Air."

NOTES

CD I gives meter signature C in all duple time sections.

Mm. 32–33, natural sign before note 2 in CD I. M. 40, natural sign before note 3 in CD I. M. 102, last two notes are quarter-notes in CD I. M. 115, syllable *ba* one note earlier in CD I. M. 158, last note has text *ron* in

CDM. M. 180, CD I has extraneous barline before eighth last note. M. 199, alternate emb is untexted pencil sketch at foot of CD I, 3; accompaniment in source B continues sixteenth-note figure of preceding four measures, but cadenzas seem to demand a full stop.

[7] *En vain j'espère*

SOURCES

A. Giacomo Meyerbeer, *Robert le diable* (Paris: Maurice Schlesinger, pl. no. 1155 [1831]; facsimile reprint with an introduction by Charles Rosen, New York: Garland, 1980).

B. Giacomo Meyerbeer, *Robert le diable . . . partition piano et chant* (Paris: Brandus, Dufour et Cie, pl. no. 9197 [ca. 1834]).

C. CDM, 96–97 [labels reported in Notes below].

CD III, 13–14, "Robert le diable" (seven numbered passages in pencil sketch).

NOTES

Source A has a text (beginning "Il me délaisse") that differs from that found in the other sources. There are chorus parts at mm. 62–92. All seven embs in CD III have a key signature of one sharp, although the notation of the last emb (mm. 197–99) assumes a key signature of four sharps.

M. 53, rhythmic pattern is eighth- plus three sixteenth-notes in CD III. M. 56, cadenza and its two alternates labelled "Point d'Orgue 1er mouvement de l'Air de Robert. (2e acte.)" in CDM. M. 190, natural sign before notes 9 and 15 in CD III. M. 200, variants labelled "Traits pour l'Air de Robert. (2e acte.)" in CDM; CDM also reproduces an untexted version of the original vocal line of mm. 200–206. M. 204, in second variant notes 9–12 are sixteenth-notes. M. 205, in first variant notes 2–5 are sixteenth-notes. M. 219, variants labelled "Dans le même Air." in CDM; all variants have text *ah* throughout and omit *coeur* under note 1. Mm. 219–20, CDM reproduces a version of the original vocal line, wherein note 1 is a quarter-note without dot, and notes 2–7 are eighth-notes; in fifth variant note 4 is a sixteenth-note. M. 220, fifth variant, natural sign before note 7. M. 231, cadenza and its alternate labelled "Point d'Orgue pour la fin du 2e mouvement. même Air." in CDM; to perform either cadenza, singer may wish to omit last note of measure preceding.

[8] *Che soave zeffiretto*

SOURCES

A. Wolfgang Amadeus Mozart, *Le nozze di Figaro*, ed. Ludwig Finscher, *Neue Ausgabe sämtlicher Werke* II/5/16 (Kassel: Bärenreiter, 1973).

C. CD III, 33–34, "Duetto (les Noces de Figaro) W. A. Mozart" (four numbered passages in ink).

CD VI, 3, "Duetto (les Noces de Figaro) W. A. Mozart" (one passage in pencil, nearly identical with CD III, 34).

NOTES

Mm. 50–51, emb may be sung instead at mm. 53–54. M. 61, in CD III notes 11–14 have descrescendo fork, notes 16–17 in Countess's part are eighth-notes, and note 27 in Countess's part is c"—edition follows CD VI.

[9] *Voi che sapete*

SOURCES

A. Wolfgang Amadeus Mozart, *Le nozze di Figaro*, ed. Ludwig Finscher, *Neue Ausgabe sämtlicher Werke* II/5/16 (Kassel: Bärenreiter, 1973).

C. CD III, 12, "Les noces de Figaro—Mon coeur soupire" (eight numbered passages in pencil with French text).

NOTES

All notes refer to readings in CD III.

M. 18, text is *dire*. Mm. 23–24, text is *si je l'osais*. Mm. 27–28, text is *raconterais*. Mm. 33–34, no text. Mm. 42–44, no text. Mm. 51–52, text is *ce que je sens*. M. 61, text is *-si*. Mm. 75–77, text is *dire si c'est d'amour*.

[10] *Dunque io son*

SOURCES

A. Gioachino Rossini, *Il barbiere di Siviglia*, ed. Alberto Zedda (Milan: Ricordi, 1969).

B. Gioachino Rossini, *The Barber of Seville*, revised from the original orchestral score by W. S. Rockstro (London: T. Boosey, [1848]).

C. Garcia, *Traité* 2:57.

Garcia, *Hints*, 65.

Marchisio, "Barbiere Duetto" (one passage in ink).

NOTES

M. 105, lower Marchisio emb, note 10 is e". Mm. 108–12, concerning the three embs presented in his *Traité*, Garcia notes that "the first figure offers more movement than the second and third, but these surpass it in the brilliance of intervals (*par le brillant des intonations*)." M. 109, upper Marchisio emb, note 4 has text *-lo*, notes 5–8 have text *amor*. M. 110, lower Marchisio emb, notes 9–11 have text *devi*.

[11] *Ecco ridente in cielo*

SOURCES

A. Gioachino Rossini, *Il barbiere di Siviglia*, ed. Alberto Zedda (Milan: Ricordi, 1969).

B. Gioachino Rossini, *The Barber of Seville*, revised from the original orchestral score by W. S. Rockstro (London: T. Boosey, [1848]).

C. Garcia, *Traité* 2:55.

NOTES

All notes refer to readings in Garcia, *Traité*.

Some accents in the edition of Garcia used here are printed with the fork opening to the right (<)—see mm. 15, 16, and 31. This peculiarity also appears in the Italian edition of the *Traité*, except that the accents in m. 15 open to the left—see *Scuola di Garcia: Trattato completo dell'arte del canto, di Emanuele Garcia figlio*, tradotto dal francese da Alberto Mazzucato (Milan: G. Ricordi, [1849?]). While the present edition follows source C above, I have not been able to determine from Garcia's treatises whether these two accent forms mean different things or are merely typographical variants. M.17, notes 2–3, breath indication reads "1/2 R." (i.e., *demi-respiration*). M. 19, note 5, the stacked *n*'s are not a mistake but a convention adopted by Garcia in the *Traité* 2:10–12 ("De l'appui des consonnes"), indicating special emphasis of the consonant. M. 25, beat 2, edition follows vertical alignment given in source—the lack of a 64th beam on the last nine notes, if not an error, may indicate a slightly freer rendition. M. 26, syllable *mi-* is under note 5—moved by analogy with text placement in mm. 17 (last four notes) and 21 (notes 4–7). M. 28, note 1 has text *oh di-* and note 2 has *-o*—edition follows Italian edition of *Traité* cited above. M. 29, next last note has ♯—moved to f" preceding. M. 30, note 1 has ♮, and note 10, ostensibly an "extra" note, may indicate a slight rubato or that the last three notes are to be sung as a triplet.

[12] *Una voce poco fu*

Source

A. Gioachino Rossini, *Il barbiere di Siviglia*, ed. Alberto Zedda (Milan: Ricordi, 1969).

B. Gioachino Rossini, *The Barber of Seville*, revised from the original orchestral score by W. S. Rockstro (London: T. Boosey, [1848]).

C. CDM, 93, "Point d'Orgue pour la Cavatine de IL BARBIERE."

Marchisio, "Barbiere" (four embellished passages with alternates, in ink).

Lind, appendix, 13–17.

Castil Blaze, 217, "Mme Gassier dans *il Barbiere*."

Notes

Cinti-Damoreau and Marchisio wrote their embellishments in E, the original key of the aria, given as [12a] in this edition. Lind wrote her embellishments in the higher transposition, F, and Gassier wrote hers yet a step higher, in G. The higher transposition is given as [12b] in this edition, with Gassier's embellishment transposed down a major second. Lind transcribed the vocal line completely, and it is such an idiosyncratic rendering that I have included it entire rather than reproducing only those measures that differ from Rossini.

[12a]—M. 39, third Marchisio emb, notes 13–14 are thirty-second notes. M. 66, the embs that end and begin in this measure are not contiguous in Marchisio but separated on the page by the emb reproduced in this edition at mm. 88–98. The continuation of the emb begins with an extraneous quarter-note b♭' on *ma* and the following upbeat figure has the text *se mi toc-*. M. 72, emb, note 7 has ♯ in Marchisio. M. 92, emb, syllable *-le* under notes 5–6, *sa-ro* under notes 7 and 8–9. M. 107, note 1, eighth-note in Marchisio embs.

[12b]—M. 16, emb, rest lacks dot. M. 31, syllable is *rò* in Lind. M. 41, text is *Sarà* in Castil-Blaze.

[13] *Nacqui all'affanno*

Sources

A. Gioachino Rossini, *La Cenerentola*, facsimile reproduction of autograph score, with an introduction by Philip Gossett (Bologna: Forni, 1978).

B. Gioachino Rossini, *Partizione della Cenerentola*, ed. L. Moreau (Paris: Launer, pl. no. 1218, [ca. 1835]).

C. CDM, 93, "Point d'Orgue pour le Rondo de la CENERENTOLA."

Pasta (Rossini autograph, nine numbered passages in ink)

Notes

There are chorus parts in mm. 45–49, and the 25-measure choral section beginning at m. 49 has been cut in this edition.

M. 12, Pasta emb, notes 6–10 are an eighth- and four thirty-second-notes, and notes 11–12 are eighth-notes; in source A, notes over *ta-* are a sixteenth-note f♯' and three thirty-second-notes b-a-b, and notes 11–15 are sixteenth-note (without trill) and four thirty-second-notes; in source B, note-groups have the pattern sixteenth-note followed by four thirty-second notes, so that measure is "too long" by a sixteenth value. M. 25, CDM emb, fourth last note undotted. M. 29, labelled "Allegro" in Pasta. M. 35, Pasta emb, notes 1 and 2 notated as dotted half-note. M. 36, emb, Pasta has extraneous quarter-note b♭'. M. 69, Pasta emb, note 9 through m. 71, note 1, not written out; marginal note specifies performance of phrase an octave higher. M. 81, Pasta emb, *starò* under notes 13–16. M. 85, Pasta emb, double sharp sign before note 1. M. 86, Pasta, the alternate is entered directly below the corresponding bar of the emb; only the alternate is underlaid with a text.

[14] *Di piacer mi balza il cor*

Sources

A. Gioachino Rossini, *La gazza ladra*, ed. Alberto Zedda, *Edizione critica delle opere*, vol. 21 (Pesaro: Fondazione Rossini, 1979).

B. Gioachino Rossini, *La gazza ladra* (Leipzig: Breitkopf & Härtel, pl. no. 3158 [1820]).

C. CD III, 1–3, "La Pie Voleuse" (one numbered passage in ink, eighteen passages in pencil—thirteen of them numbered, two of them alternates—and four additional passages labelled "autres traits p⟨ou⟩r le même air").

Notes

All notes refer to readings in CD III.

M. 38, first emb staff, sharp before note 5. Mm. 38–40, [*autre*] emb found on p. 3 of source among "autres traits p⟨ou⟩r le même air"; sign after last note may mean that emb is to be continued as in either of the other embs. M. 88, sharp before note 11. Mm. 108–10, either emb could be sung in mm. 106–8. Mm. 130–32, emb found on p. 3 of source among "autres traits p⟨ou⟩r le même air."

[15] *Sombre forêt*

SOURCES

A. Gioachino Rossini, *Guillaume Tell* (Paris: Troupenas, 1829–30; facsimile reprint with an introduction by Philip Gossett, New York: Garland, 1980).

B. Gioachino Rossini, *Guillaume Tell* (Paris: Troupenas, pl. no. E.T. et Cie 2323 [ca. 1850]).

C. CDM, 94–95, "Point d'Orgue pour la Romance de GUILLAUME TELL" (five alternate cadenzas).

[16] *Pensa alla patria*

SOURCES

A. Gioachino Rossini, *L'italiana in Algeri*, ed. Azio Corghi, *Edizione critica delle opere*, vol. 11 (Pesaro: Fondazione Rossini, 1981).

B. Gioachino Rossini, *Partition de L'Italienne à Alger* (Paris: Carli, pl. no. 1188 [1821–22]).

C. CD II, 7–9, "Air de L'Italienne à Alger introduit dans Otello. / (Ô jour prospère.)" (fifteen numbered passages in ink).

NOTES

There are chorus parts at mm. 50–51, 54–55, 57–64, 92–105, and 122–48.

Cinti-Damoreau's inscription indicates that she included this aria in her performances of Rossini's *Otello*, probably with the French text that appears in this source. I have been unable to locate the complete text used by Cinti-Damoreau, so an editorial underlay of the Italian text is proposed in this edition for her ornaments. All notes refer to the readings of CD II.

M. 45, notes 1 and 2 are sixteenth-notes. Mm. 113–15, no text in source. M. 118, notes 1–6 have text *châines*. M. 119, notes 1–3 have text *chaine*. M. 131, notes 1–4 have text *châines*. M. 147, note 10 has letter *o*, apparently a false start at *orgueil*.

[17] *Parlar, spiegar*

SOURCES

A. Gioachino Rossini, *Mosè in Egitto*, facsimile reproduction of autograph score, with an introduction by Philip Gossett (New York: Garland, 1979).

B. Gioachino Rossini, *Moïse* (Paris: Brandus & Cie, pl. no. E.T. & Cie 2121 [1851]).

C. Castil-Blaze, 216–17, "*Mosè*, 1832–42" (two vocal staves, labelled "Rubini"and "Tamburini," corresponding to mm. 95–161; the vocal lines are identical with those of source B in mm. 95–99, 103–5, 107–10, 144–46, 149–55, and 157).

NOTES

M. 156, emb, notes 5–8 have text *-pido*; notes 9–12 have text *a*.

[18] "*Assisa a piè*"

SOURCES

A. Gioachino Rossini, *Otello*, facsimile reproduction of autograph score, with an introduction by Philip Gossett (New York: Garland, 1979).

B. Gioachino Rossini, *Otello; ossia, L'africano di Venezia*, ridotto per il piano-forte (Paris: Boieldieu, pl. no. 988 [1820–21]).

C. CD II, 55, "Otello. Romance du Saule" (nine numbered passages in pencil and one unnumbered sketch).

NOTES

All notes refer to readings in CD II.

Mm. 42–43, alternate passage [*autre*?] lightly sketched on same staff as emb, in m. 42 notes 5–8 are beamed as sixteenth-notes, and in m. 43 notes 1 and 5–8 are beamed as sixteenth-notes. M. 58, note is unflagged; this emb (extending into m. 60) is an untexted, barely decipherable sketch at bottom of page. M. 60, lower emb, note 3 is a sixteenth-note, and the rest is an eighth-rest. M. 90, syllables *-si accen-* appear under notes 12–14. M. 141, emb written in doubled rhythmic values, with *al-* under note 1 and *-me-* under note 3. This and subsequent emb are notated with a key signature of two flats. M. 144, emb written in doubled rhythmic values, with a barline before note 10, and note 17 has a sharp sign.

[19] *Ah, quel giorno ognor rammento*

SOURCES

A. Gioachino Rossini, *Semiramide*, facsimile reproduction of autograph score, with an introduction by Philip Gossett (New York: Garland, 1978).

B. Gioachino Rossini, *Sémiramis* (Paris: Heugel, pl. no. H2649 [1860]).

C. CD II, 9–11, "Sémiramide air d'Arsace" (fourteen numbered passages in ink).

NOTES

All notes refer to readings in CD II. On either side of the title are two parenthetical notes. The first—"(introduit dans Otello)"—indicates that Cinti-Damoreau sang this aria (as she did "Pensa alla patria" [16] from *L'italiana in Algeri*) in her performances of Rossini's *Otello*. The second—"(Il revient celui que j'aime)"—is probably the incipit of the text she used for this aria. I have been unable to locate the complete text; nineteenth-century French translations of the libretto of *Semiramide* give this aria a text beginning "O bonheur de l'âme ravie." An editorial underlay of the Italian text is proposed in this edition for her embellishments.

M. 33, note 2 is unflagged. M. 92, no text. M. 98, eighth-rest and half-note are reversed. M. 122, second last note is dotted, which may indicate that Cinti-Damoreau wished a slight lengthening of this note in performance.

[20] *Du séjour de la lumière*

SOURCES

A. Gioachino Rossini, *Le siège de Corinthe* (Paris: Troupenas, 1826–27; facsimile reprint with an introduction by Philip Gossett, New York: Garland, 1980).

B. Gioachino Rossini, *Le siège de Corinthe* (Vienna: T. Haslinger, pl. no. T.H. 4960–4974 [1827–30]).

C. CD II, 16–17, "Le Siège de Corinthe" (ten numbered passages in ink, two pencilled sketches, also numbered).

NOTES

There are choruses following m. 44 (32 mm.) and the downbeat of m. 73 (21 mm.)—these sections have been cut in this edition. There are choral parts from m. 100 to m. 118.

M. 20, emb marked "Andante" in CD II. M. 27, emb, note 1 has extraneous sharp sign, and notes 11 and 17 have flat signs, in CD II. M. 29, emb, notes 1 and 2 have text *-las* in pencil rather than ink in CD II. M. 30, emb, note 4 has extraneous sharp sign in CD II. M. 31, emb, notes 12 and 13 in pencil in CD II. M. 35, CD II has text *-tin* without pitch. M. 45, marked "Meno mosso" in sources A and B, since choral Allegro has intervened. M. 54, emb marked "Allegro" in CD II.

[21] *Di tanti palpiti*

SOURCES

A. Gioachino Rossini, *Tancredi*, ed. Philip Gossett, *Edizione critica delle opere*, vol. 10/2 (Pesaro: Fondazione Rossini, 1984).

B. Gioachino Rossini, *Tancredi*, ridotta per pianoforte solo da Luigi Truzzi (Milan: Ricordi, n.d.).

C. Gregoire (Rossini autograph giving embellished transcription of vocal line for recitative and four numbered passages for aria, with orchestral passages in piano reduction; see plate 4).

Anonymous (piano-vocal score of entire aria, showing embellishments in cue-size notation on the vocal staff; see plate 5).

CD II, 44–46, "Tancrède O patrie" (sixteen numbered passages and one alternate in pencil, with French text).

Pasta, in CD IV, 21, "Tancredi. Points d'Orgue et traits de Mme Pasta, dans l'air de Tancredi qu'elle chantait *inimitablement!*" (two numbered passages in pencil).

NOTES

Anonymous, CD II, and Pasta are all written in the key of D through the recitative and in the key of G from the Maestoso; they are transposed in this edition. The number of embellishment sources for this aria makes it desirable to report on each source separately.

Gregoire. The barring and rhythmic values diverge considerably in the recitative from those of source A, but since this source has Rossini's authority, the edition follows it as exactly as possible, showing by vertical alignment the correspondence with the unembellished vocal line. This autograph gives cues in piano reduction for the accompaniment at mm. 23–24, 27–28, 30, 32–36, 38–40, 44–46, 48, and 49–51; these are not included in this edition. Also suppressed are the designations *Canto*, *Piano*, *Recit.*, and *Aria*.

M. 40, beat 1 is eighth-note f" (last note of accompaniment cue followed by eighth-rest. M. 44, accompaniment cue begins only after end of vocal line; in performance of this emb staff, the pianist should wait until the singer has finished. M. 58, extraneous triplet sign over note 7. M. 94, note 1 undotted. M. 101, note 1 and syllable *Sa-* given as cue. M. 129, notes 1 and 7 are eighth-notes.

Anonymous. The piano introduction has only the accompaniment figure in common with the introduction in sources A and B and is eight measures shorter besides. This source also proceeds rather differently in the Allegro corresponding to mm. 33–52 of this edition: it has different harmonies and five fewer measures.

M. 103, notes 2 and 6 and thirty-second beams printed full-size. M. 137, source omits the music of this measure.

CD II. The complete French text used by Cinti-Damoreau has been found in no other source. An editorial underlay of the Italian text is proposed for her embellishments.

M. 32, note 4 has text *-nâi-*. M. 58, notes 5–8 are sixteenth-notes. Mm. 62–64, *autre* emb has no text except for *vainqueur* under last two notes. M. 87, marked "Allegro." M. 95, extraneous barline before last note. M. 115, extraneous barline between notes 1 and 2, note 1 has text *charme*, and notes 2–4 have no text. M. 126, edition follows the inexact notation of the source, but vertical alignment suggests proper rhythm. M. 135, note 1 is quarter-note.

Pasta. M. 62, note 11 has natural sign. M. 63, last two notes of bar have text *va-lor*.

[22] *Lasciami: non t'ascolto*

SOURCES

A. Gioachino Rossini, *Tancredi*, ed. Philip Gossett, *Edizione critica delle opere*, vol. 10/2 (Pesaro: Fondazione Rossini, 1984).

B. Gioachino Rossini, *Tancredi*, ridotta per pianoforte solo da Luigi Truzzi (Milan: Ricordi, n.d.).

C. Pasta (Rossini autograph, in ink, giving embellished transcription of Tancredi's first speech).

CD III, 8, "Tancrède – duo" (two numbered passages in pencil).

NOTES

Pasta has neither clef nor key signature but implies soprano clef and three flats. Apart from one minor variant in Pasta for mm. 147–51 (shown in source A, p. 607), neither embellishment source presents any passages for the section of the Allegro beginning "Sì tu sol crudel"; rather than reproduce this music, the edition cuts from m. 133 to m. 221 of the duet, which can be supplied by any piano-vocal score.

M. 18, Pasta emb, slur covers only notes 4–8.

Acknowledgments

I am indebted to many individuals who have helped in differing ways to get this complex project into print. William Cagle and the staff of the Lilly Library of Indiana University have been invariably helpful, as have been Rigbie Turner and the staff of the Pierpont Morgan Library of New York. Thanks go to both of these libraries for permission to edit and reproduce their materials for this edition. I am most grateful to Steven M. Whiting of A-R Editions for his careful and solicitous shepherding of edition and author through times when solutions were invisible.

Austin B. Caswell

Notes

1. See, as examples, the following recent studies: Daniel J. Koury, *Orchestral Performance Practices in the Nineteenth Century: Size, Proportions, and Seating* (Ann Arbor: UMI Research Press, 1986); Robert Winter, "The Emperor's New Clothes: Nineteenth-Century Instruments Revisited," *Nineteenth-Century Music* 7 (1984): 251–65; Harold C. Schonberg, *The Glorious Ones: Classical Music's Legendary Performers* (New York: New York Times Books, 1985); Jurgen Thym, ed., *100 Years of Eichendorff Songs*, Recent Researches in the Music of the Nineteenth and Early Twentieth Centuries, vol. 5 (Madison: A-R Editions, Inc., 1983); and Will Crutchfield, "Vocal Ornamentation in Verdi: The Phonographic Evidence," *Nineteenth-Century Music* 7 (1983): 3–54.

2. See, for example, Crutchfield, "Vocal Ornamentation."

3. Castil-Blaze [François Henri Joseph Blaze], *Théâtres lyriques de Paris: L'Académie Impériale de Musique de 1645 à 1855*, 2 vols. (Paris: Castil-Blaze, 1855), 2:202. This and all subsequent translations have been made by the present writer.

4. Donald J. Grout, *A Short History of Opera*, 2d ed. (New York: Columbia University Press, 1965), 331.

5. Ibid., 354.

6. For an account of her career, see Austin Caswell, "Mme Cinti-Damoreau and the Embellishment of Italian Opera in Paris: 1820–1845," *Journal of the American Musicological Society* 28 (1975): 460–70.

7. "On doit varier une pensée chaque fois qu'elle se répète." Garcia, *Traité* 2:56; for a full bibliographic citation, see Sources.

8. "Le sens des paroles détermine . . . les ornements et le caractère que comporte l'exécution." Garcia, *Traité* 2:57.

9. "Nous ne nous permettons pas, nous autres Français, de respirer au milieu d'un mot, de répéter une syllabe, . . . enfins nous ne devons pas sacrifier les paroles aux notes, mais bien au contraire sacrifier les notes aux paroles." Cinti-Damoreau, *Méthode*, 1; for a full bibliographic citation, see Sources.

10. "Je ne vous les donne pas, d'ailleurs, pour que vous les exécutiez à tout prix, en dépit même de votre organisation et de votre nature. Ce sont des formules variées que je vous propose, pour que, plus tard, votre goût vous amène, dans la limite de vos moyens, à en trouver d'autres qui vous appartiennent en propre." Cinti-Damoreau, *Méthode*, 2.

11. Translated from the dedication on the title page of Marchisio, "Cadenze"; for a full bibliographic citation, see Sources. The original text of the dedication—to R. E. Pagliari, librarian of the Royal Conservatory in Naples—reads as follows:

Buen amico,

Offrò a voi questi cari ricordi della fortunata la mia carriera, a voi che avete ancora raccolti gli ultimi sospiri, gli sprazzi i resti dal nostro bel canto Italiano. E non ve li offro nò nel merito loro ne colla più lontana speranza che passano un giorno essere utili alle giovane alunne di questo vostro conservatorio.

Oh! no, amico mio, ogni giorno di più mi convinco che oggi chi aspira all'arte mia adorata segue tutti altra via con troppo frette e minore entusiasmo! Ve li offrò questa volta per la sola certezza che gelosamente voi conserverete le brevi composizioni che vi ricordano il connubio canaro delle sorelle fortunate, perche ben vecchia e mai stanca, avete conscinta una delle esecutrici sogliencola ai dolci riposi e spronandola all'insegnamento.

Sempre vostra affezionatissima

Barbara Marchisio
27 Giugno 1900

12. Philip Gossett, "The Operas of Rossini: Problems of Textual Criticism in Nineteenth-Century Opera" (Ph.D. diss., Princeton University, 1970).

13. For further information about these sources, including a complete inventory, see Caswell, "Mme Cinti-Damoreau and Embellishment," 470–81.

14. Luigi Ricci, *Variazioni-cadenze tradizioni per canto* (Milan: Ricordi, 1937), vol. 1, *Voci femminili*.

15. See Gioachino Rossini, *Tancredi*, ed. Philip Gossett, *Edizione critica delle opere*, vol. 10/2 (Pesaro: Fondazione Rossini, 1984), 602–7, as well as the accompanying *Commento Critico*, 199–200.

16. Clementi and Co. were active at 26 Cheapside in London over an extended period, but Tyson and Neighbour indicate that the firm began a regular series of plate numbers only in 1828. Since this print has no plate number, and since the watermark on the first sheet consists of the date 1821, it was probably issued between 1821 and 1828. See Oliver Neighbour and Alan Tyson, *English Music Publishers' Plate Numbers in the First Half of the Nineteenth Century* (London: Faber & Faber, 1965), 22–23. The two sets of page numbers in this print—one beginning with 95 at the center of the top margin and the other beginning with 1 in the top right corner—reflect yet another publishing practice of the time: that of selling sheet music either bound in anthologies or as single items. This particular copy (in the editor's possession) appears to have been part of a bound anthology at one time, since fragments of dried glue and paper are still attached to the edge.

17. Many libretti have been reprinted, without scholarly commentary or editorial examination, in the ongoing series English and American Drama of the Nineteenth Century (New York: Readex Microprint Co.). Texts for which reprints in this series have been consulted are those for arias [2], [3], [7], [13], [15], [17], and [19].

18. "Les morceaux qui reposent sur le retour d'un motif . . . sont particulièrement destinées à recevoir des changements. Ces changements, dans leur disposition, doivent suivre une progression croissante." Garcia, *Traité* 2:56.

19. See Gioachino Rossini, *Il barbiere di Siviglia*, ed. Alberto Zedda (Milan: Ricordi, 1969), 19.

20. This dating is corroborated by Thomas F. Heck, "Ricordi Plate Numbers in the Earlier Nineteenth Century: A Chronological Survey," *Current Musicology*, no. 10 (1970): 117; and by Agostina Zecca-Laterza, *Il catalogo numerico Ricordi 1857* (Rome: Nuovo Istituto Editoriale Italiano, 1984).

Texts and Translations

Texts and translations are presented for each aria according to procedures described under Editorial Methods, above. As a rule, the texts are drawn from the aria sources identified in the Critical Notes. Exceptions to this rule have been made for arias [5], [7], and [13], where early piano-vocal scores (identified as source B in the Critical Notes) have been preferred to orchestral scores. Any additional sources consulted for the regularization of spelling, punctuation, and line division, are listed below with their respective texts.

[1] Ma la sola

Ma la sola, ohimè! son io,
che penar per lui si veda?
O mie genti! O suol natio!
di chi mai vi diedi in preda?
Ed io stessa, ed io potei
soggettarvi a un tal signor?
O mio rossor!

Ah! la pena in lor piombò
dell'amor che mi perdè;
i martir dovuti a me
il destin a lor serbò.

Muse in ciel sperar si può
un sol raggio di pietà,
la costanza a noi darà.
se la pace ne involò.

But alas, am I the only one
who should see herself suffer because of him?
O my people! O native soil!
unto whom have I given you as prey?
And I myself—and I could
subject you to such a lord as this?
Oh, my shame!

Ah! On them has fallen the pain
of the love that ruined me;
the sufferings due me
fate reserved for them.

Muses in heaven, if one can hope
for a single ray of mercy,
it will grant us steadfastness,
though it has stolen our peace.

[2] Ah! non credea mirarti

Ah! non credea mirarti
sì presto estinto, O fiore;
passasti al par d'amore,
che un giorno solo durò.

Potria novel vigore
il pianto mio recarti,
ma ravvivar l'amore
il pianto mio non può!

Ah, I did not expect to see you
dead so soon, O flower;
you have faded like love,
which lasted only one day.

Perhaps my tears could
restore you to new vigor,
but revive love,
that my tears cannot do!

SOURCE: *La sonnambula* . . . , the libretto edited and translated by Manfredo Maggioni (London: T. Brettell, [1848?]).

[3] Come per me sereno

Care compagne, e voi teneri amici,
che alla gioia mia tanta parte prendete,
Oh! come dolci scendon d'Amina al core
i canti che v'inspira il vostro amore!

A te, diletta, tenera madre,
che a sì lieto giorno
me orfanella serbasti,
a te favelli questo,
dal cor più che dal ciglio espresso,
dolce pianto di gioia, e questo amplesso.
Compagne . . . teneri amici . . .
ah madre, ah qual gioia!

    Come per me sereno
    oggi rinacque il dì!
    Come il terren fiorì
    più bello e ameno!

Dear companions and you tender friends,
who share such a great part of my joy,
oh, how sweetly fall on Amina's heart
the songs your love inspires.

To you, beloved, tender mother,
who for this happy day
saved me, an orphan,
to you let speak
these tears of joy, shed more from my heart
than from my eyes, and this embrace.
Companions . . . dear friends . . .
ah mother, ah what joy!

How peacefully for me
this day dawns anew!
How the earth blooms
more lovely and more fair!

Mai di più lieto aspetto	With happier countenance
natura non brillò:	nature was never aglow:
amor la colorò	love has colored it
del mio diletto.	with my delight.
Sovra il sen la man mi posa;	Place your hand on my breast,
palpitar, balzar lo senti;	feel how it throbs and leaps;
egli è il cor che i suoi contenti	it is my heart
non ha forza a sostener.	that cannot bear such happiness.

SOURCE: *La sonnambula . . .*, the libretto edited and translated by Manfredo Maggioni (London: Brettell, [1848?]).

[4] De tous les pays

De tous les pays, pour vous plaire,	I will know how to assume, one by one,
Je saurai prendre, tour à tour,	the traits and the character
Les goûts et le caractère.	of each country, just to please you.
A la Française vive et légère,	Would you like to devote your love and attention
Voulez-vous consacrer vos soins et votre amour?	to a French girl, lively and light-hearted?
D'une flamme si belle,	To pay the price for you
Pour vous payer le prix,	of such a lovely flame,
Je vous serai fidèle . . .	I will be faithful to you . . .
Comme on l'est à Paris.	as one is in Paris.
Du chant italien si vous êtes épris,	If you are charmed by Italian songs,
Du ton le plus lamentable,	in the most pitiable tone,
Je vous peindrai mon ardeur	I will portray for you my ardor
Et l'excès de la douleur	and the excess of grief
Qui, loin de vous, m'accable.	that oppresses me when far from you.
Si l'amour espagnol vous parait préférable,	If Spanish love seems preferable to you,
Je vous attends, dans l'ombre de la nuit;	I will wait for you in the shadows of the night;
Loin des jaloux, nous nous verrons sans bruit.	far from the envious, we will gaze at each other in silence.
Faudra-t'il imiter la plaintive Ecossaise?	Must I imitate the plaintive Scot?
Sur le sommet des monts, je ferai, nuit et jour,	From the mountain tops I will make echo
Répéter aux échos tendres soupirs d'amour.	night and day the tender sighs of love.
A mon époux, pour peu que l'Allemande plaise,	For my husband, little though a German girl may please him,
Comme elle, on me verra valser,	you will see me waltz like her,
Tourner, passer et repasser.	turn, step, and step again.
Si pour compagne enfin, vous voulez une Anglaise,	If, finally, you should choose an English girl for a partner,
Vous verrez, qu'oubliant	you will find that, disregarding
Parfois leur indolence,	their occasional laziness,
Il règne dans leur danse	their dance has
Un aimable enjoument.	a certain playfulness.
Violà par quelle heureuse adresse,	There you see by what happy shrewdness
Fixant l'objet de ma tendresse,	holding fast the object of my love,
Mon époux, suivant mes désirs,	my husband, following my own desires.
Chaque jour, sans être infidèle,	every day, without being unfaithful,
Auprès d'une femme nouvelle,	will taste new pleasures
Goûtera de nouveaux plaisirs.	with a new woman.

SOURCE: [François-Adrien] Boieldieu, *Le calife de Bagdad: Opéra en un acte, représenté, sur le Théâtre Favart, le 29 Fructidor an VIII. Paroles de S. Just . . .*, seconde édition (Paris, Vente An XI [1802/3]).

[5] Comme aux jours

Enfin je vous revois, séjour de mon enfance.	At last I see you again, haven of my childhood.
Pour mon coeur quelle jouissance.	What joy to my heart.
Et vous, mes nobles protecteurs,	And you, my noble protectors,
Du haut des cieux, qui sont votre partage,	from the heights of heaven, your abode,
Vous n'avez pas permis que ce bel héritage	you have not allowed this beautiful heritage
Retombât dans les mains d'indignes ravisseurs.	to fall back into the hands of unworthy despoilers.
Comme aux jours de mon jeune âge,	As in the days of my youth,

Daignez encor, daignez guider mes pas.
Comme aux jours de mon jeune âge,
Veillez sur moi, ne m'abandonnez pas.
En revoyant ce noble asile
De mon bonheur, je me souviens
Que de fois ce séjour tranquille
A redit le nom de Julien.
L'écho fidèle ne l'a point oublié,
Il me rappelle nos jeux, notre amitié.

[6] Non, je ne veux pas chanter

Non, je ne veux pas chanter.
Vous pouvez bien m'écouter.
Mais non, je ne veux pas chanter.

Que voulez-vous que je vous chante?
Est-ce un air simple et gracieux,
Qui vous captive et vous enchante
Par des accents mélodieux?

Chanterai-je un rondeau facile
Qui fasse naître la gaieté?
Et partout comme un vaudeville
Soit retenu, soit répété?

Mais non, je ne veux pas chanter. . . .

Au temps passé, dans plaintive romance
On soupirait tendres accents d'amour.
Au temps présent, pour charmer sa souffrance,
L'amant redit les chants du troubadour.

Mais non, tout me le persuade,
Et je le vois bien à vos yeux,
Et la cadence et la roulade
Sont ce que vous aimez le mieux.
Par malheur j'ai peu de science
Sur la roulade et la cadence.

Non, je ne veux pas chanter. . . .

[7] En vain j'espère

(Isabelle)

En vain j'espère
Un sort prospère;
Douce chimère,
Rêves d'amour,
Avez fui sans retour!

D'espoir bercée,
Tendre pensée
S'est éclipsée
Comme un beau jour.

(Alice)

Dieu! si j'osais . . .
Mais les dames, dit-on,
et les Princesses même
reçoivent quelquefois
de semblables placets!
Essayons!

(Isabelle)

Ciel! que vois-je!
C'est de Robert!
En croirais-je mes yeux?

---

deign still, deign to guide my steps.
As in the days of my youth,
watch over me, do not desert me.
Looking again on this noble refuge
of my happiness, I recall
how many times this peaceful haven
repeated the name of Julian.
The faithful echo has not forgotten it,
it reminds me of our games, our affection.

No, I do not wish to sing.
You can listen to me all you want,
but no, I do not wish to sing.

What do you want me to sing for you?
Is it a simple and pleasant air,
which captivates and enchants you
by its melodious accents?

Shall I sing an easy rondo
that causes merriment
And like a vaudeville
is everywhere retained and repeated?

But no, I do not wish to sing. . . .

In times past, one sighed
tender accents of love into plaintive romances.
In present times, the lover repeats
the troubadour's songs to beguile his suffering.

But no, everything convinces me,
and I see clearly in your eyes:
the cadenza and the roulade
are what you like the most.
Unfortunately I have little knowledge
about the roulade and the cadenza.

No, I do not wish to sing. . . .

In vain I hope
for a favorable fate;
Sweet vision,
dreams of love,
you have fled beyond return!

Cradled by hope,
the tender thought
has vanished
like a beautiful day.

God! if I dared . . .
But the ladies, so they say,
and even the princesses
sometimes receive
similar petitions!
Let us try!

Heavens! what do I see!
It is from Robert!
Should I believe my eyes?

Idole de ma vie,
Ah! viens,
Mon âme est attendrie!
Le malheur qui supplie
A des droits sur mon coeur!

Ah Robert!
Mon bonheur est extrême!
Robert, viens, toi que j'aime!

Idol of my life,
ah, come,
my heart is softened!
Suppliant misery
has a claim on my heart!

Ah, Robert!
My joy is extreme!
Robert, come, you whom I love!

[8] Che soave zeffiretto

(Canzonetta sull'aria)

Che soave zeffiretto
  (zeffiretto . . .)
questa sera spirerà,
  (questa sera spirerà . . .)
sotto i pini del boschetto,
  (sotto i pini del boschetto . . .)
ei già il resto capirà.
  (certo il capirà.)

"What a gentle breeze

will blow this evening

beneath the pines of the grove,"

and the rest he will understand.

[9] Voi che sapete

Voi che sapete che cosa è amor,
donne, vedete s'io l'ho nel cor.
Quello ch'io provo vi ridirò,
è per me nuovo, capir nol so.

Sento un affetto pien di desir,
ch'ora è diletto, ch'ora è martir.
Gelo e poi sento l'alma avvampar,
e in un momento torno a gelar.

Ricerco un bene fuori di me,
non so ch'il tiene, non so cos'è.
Sospiro e gemo senza voler,
palpito e tremo senza saper.
Non trovo pace notte ne dì,
ma pur mi piace languir così.

You who know what love is,
women, see if I have it in my heart.
I ask you to tell me what it is I feel;
it is new to me, I cannot understand it.

I feel a sensation filled with desire,
which is now a delight, then a torment.
I freeze and then feel my soul aflame,
and in a moment I turn back to ice.

I seek a happiness outside of myself,
I do not know what it holds, nor what it is.
I sigh and groan without control,
I shake and tremble without knowing it.
I get no rest night or day,
but still this misery pleases me so.

[10] Dunque io son

Ros: Dunque io son . . . tu non m'inganni?
  Dunque io son . . . la fortunata!
  (Già me l'ero immaginata:
  lo sapevo pria di te.)

Fig: Di Lindoro il vago oggetto
  siete voi, bella Rosina.
  (Oh che volpe soprafina!
  ma l'avrà da far con me.)

Ros: Senti, senti . . . ma a Lindoro
  per parlar come si fa?

Fig: Zitto, zitto, qui Lindoro
  per parlarvi or or sarà.

Ros: Per parlarmi? . . . Bravo! bravo!
  Venga pur, ma con prudenza;
  io già moro d'impazienza!
  Ma che tarda, cosa fa?

Fig: Egli attende qualche segno,
  poverin, del vostro affetto;
  sol due righe di biglietto,
  gli mandate e qui verrà.
  Che ne dite?

Then I am . . . you're not fooling me?
Then I am . . . the lucky one!
(I already guessed I would be:
I knew it before you did.)

The charming object of Lindoro's desire
is you, beautiful Rosina,
(Oh, what a superb vixen!
But she will have to deal with me.)

Listen, listen . . . but what should
I say to Lindoro?

Quiet, quiet, Lindoro
is coming to talk to you now,

To talk to me? Wonderful!
Come then, but cautiously;
I am dying of impatience!
What's the delay?

He is waiting for some sign,
poor fellow, of your affection;
send him a two-line note,
and he'll appear.
What do you say?

Ros: Non vorrei . . .

Fig: Su, coraggio.

Ros: Non saprei . . .

Fig: Sol due righe . . .

Ros: Mi vergogno . . .

Fig: Ma di che? si sa!
   Presto, presto, qua il biglietto.

Ros: Un biglietto? . . . eccolo qua.

Fig: Già era scritto! . . . ve' che bestia!
   Il maestro faccio a lei!

Ros: Fortunati affetti miei,
   io comincio a respirar.

Fig: Ah che in cattedra costei
   di malizia può dettar.

Ros: Ah tu solo, amor, tu sei
   che mi devi consolar.

Fig: Donne, donne, eterni Dei,
   chi v'arriva a indovinar?

I can't . . .

Come on, courage.

I wouldn't know how . . .

Just two lines . . .

I'm ashamed . . .

Of what? Who will know?
Quick, quick, the note.

A note? . . . here it is.

Already written! . . . How stupid I am!
As if I could teach her anything!

I feel my luck is holding,
I am beginning to breathe.

This woman is a professional
at contriving evil.

You alone, love,
can console me.

Women, women, eternal Gods,
who can fathom them?

[11] Ecco ridente in cielo

Ecco ridente in cielo
spunta la bella aurora,
e tu non sorgi ancora
e puoi dormir così?

Sorgi, mia dolce speme,
vieni, bell'idol mio,
rendi men crudo, oh Dio!
lo stral che mi ferì.

There, smiling in the heavens
rises the beautiful dawn,
and you have not arisen yet
and are able to sleep still?

Arise, my sweet desire,
come, my beautiful idol,
make less cruel, O God,
the arrow that wounds me.

[12] Una voce poco fa

Una voce poco fa
qui nel cor mi risuonò;
il mio cor ferito è già,
e Lindor fù che il piagò.
   Sì, Lindoro mio sarà,
   lo giurai, la vincerò,

Il tutor ricuserà,
io l'ingegno aguzzerò,
alla fin s'accheterà,
e contenta io resterò.
   Sì, Lindoro mio sarà,
   lo giurai, la vincerò.

Io sono docile, son rispettosa,
sono ubbidiente, dolce, amorosa,
mi lascio reggere, mi fò guidar.

Ma se mi toccano dov'è il mio debole,
sarò una vipera, e cento trappole
prima di cedere farò giocar.

The voice I heard just now
rings in my heart;
my heart is already struck,
and Lindoro is the one who wounded it.
   Yes, Lindoro will be mine,
   I swear it, I will win.

My guardian will object,
I will sharpen my wits,
in the end he will give in,
And I will be satisfied.
   Yes, Lindoro will be mine,
   I swear it, I will win.

I am meek, I am respectful.
I am obedient, gentle, loving,
I let myself be ruled and guided.

But if they touch me in a tender spot,
I will become a snake, and I will play
a hundred tricks before giving in.

[13] Nacqui all'affanno

Nacqui all'affanno e al pianto
soffrì tacendo il core;
ma per soave incanto
dell'età mia nel fiore,

Born to sorrow and tears,
my heart suffered in silence;
but through some gentle magic
at the time of my blossoming,

come un baleno rapido	my fate changed
la sorte mia cangiò.	like a bolt of lightning.
No, no! tergete il ciglio,	No, no! dry your tears;
perché tremar, perché?	why tremble, why?
A questo sen volate,	Fly to this breast;
figlia, sorella, amica,	daughter, sister, friend—
tutto trovate in me.	you shall find all in me.
Non più mesta accanto al fuoco	No longer shall I stay sadly by the fire,
starò sola a gorgheggiar.	singing alone.
Ah, fu un lampo, un sogno, un gioco	Ah, my long throbbing was a vision,
il mio lungo palpitar.	a dream, a trick.

[14] Di piacer me balza il cor

Di piacer mi balza il cor;	My heart leaps for joy.
ah! bramar di più non so:	Ah! I cannot wish for more:
e l'amante e il genitor	both my beloved and my father
finalmente io rivedrò.	I will see again at last.
L'uno al sen mi stringerà;	One will press me to his breast;
l'altro, ah! che farà?	The other—ah, what will he do?
Dio d'amor, confido in te;	God of love, I trust in you;
deh, tu premia la mia fè!	pray reward my faith!
Tutto sorridere mi veggo intorno;	Everything I see around me smiles;
più lieto giorno brillar non può.	a brighter day could not shine.
Ah! già dimentico i miei tormenti:	Ah! I forget my torments already.
quanti contenti alfin godrò!	What happiness I feel at last!

Cinti-Damoreau's embellishments make clear that she sang a French version of the above text closely resembling the translation made by Castil-Blaze. For singers who may wish to sing the entire aria in French, that translation is reproduced here from a contemporaneous American print, *La pie voleuse: Opéra en trois actes sur la musique de Rossini par M. Castil-Blaze* (Baltimore: E. J. Coale, 1831). This print, by the way, also gives an English rendering of Castil-Blaze's text, "translated literally for visitors to the French Opera."

> Ah, j'éprouve en ce moment
> Du bonheur l'aimable ivresse;
> Ce jour rend à ma tendresse
> Et mon père et mon amant.
> Sur son coeur l'un me pressera,
> Dans mes bras l'autre volera.
> Tendre amour, je t'implore!
> Mon âme s'abandonne a toi.
> Fais que celui que j'adore
> M'ait gardé son coeur et sa foi.
>
> Une journée si fortunée,
> Est destinée aux doux plaisirs.
> Non, plus de peines, plus de tristesse,
> Ce jour les rend à ma tendresse,
> Tout vient sourire à mes désirs.

Cinti-Damoreau's text diverges from the above French version in the cabaletta, where only the following fragmentary verse can be reconstructed from her embellishments:

> Oui, tout m'enchante; jamais l'attente
> Pour une amante . . .
> Non, plus de peines, plus de tristesse,
> [Ce jour les rend à ma] tendresse,
> Puis-je former d'autres souhaits.

[15] Sombre forêt

Sombre forêt, désert triste et sauvage,	Dark forest, wild and dismal wilderness,
Je vous préfère aux splendeurs des palais:	I prefer you to the splendors of palaces;
C'est sur les monts, au séjour de l'orage,	it is on the mountains, in the home of the storm,
Que mon coeur peut renaître à la paix;	that my heart can recover its peace;
Mais l'écho seulement apprendra mes secrets.	but the echo alone shall know my secrets.

Toi, du berger astre doux et timide,
Qui sur mes pas viens semant tes reflets,
Ah, sois aussi mon étoile et mon guide.
Comme lui, tes rayons sont discrets;
Et l'écho seulement redira mes secrets.

You shy and gentle star of the shepherd,
Who comes to shed your light on my steps,
ah, be also my beacon and my guide.
Like him, your rays are discreet;
and the echo alone will repeat my secrets.

[16] Pensa alla patria

Pensa alla patria, e intrepido
il tuo dovere adempi:

    vedi per tutta Italia
    rinascere gli esempi
    d'ardire e di valor.

Sciocco! tu ridi ancora?
Vanne, mi fai dispetto.
Caro, ti parli in petto
amore, dovere, onor.
Amici in ogni evento . . .
Vicino è già il momento . . .
Se poi va male il gioco . . .

    Qual piacer! Fra pochi istanti
    rivedrem le patrie arene.
    (Nel periglio del mio bene
    coraggiosa amor mi fa.)

Think of your country, and bravely
fulfill your duty:

    see, throughout all Italy
    examples of boldness
    and valor are reborn.

Fool! Are you still laughing?
Go away, you annoy me.
Dearest, in your heart may
love, duty, and honor speak to you.
Friends no matter what happens . . .
The moment is already near . . .
But if the plan goes badly . . .

    What delight! in a few moments
    we will see our homeland's shore.
    (In the danger of my dear one,
    love makes me brave.)

Concerning the text of Cinti-Damoreau's embellishments, see the Critical Notes for this aria.

[17] Parlar, spiegar

Os: Parlar, spiegar non posso
    quel che nel petto io sento.
    Ah! no . . . del mio tormento
    darsi non può maggior!

Fa: È il ciel per noi sereno,
    se pria fu avverso e fiero:
    Ti calmerà, sì lo spero,
    dolce e soave amor.

Os: No . . . sempre sventurato . . .

Fa: Perchè? Qual tristo evento?

Os: Padre! Ah! non sai . . .

Fa: Favella . . .

Os: La mia nemica stella
    mi vuole oppresso ognor.

Fa: È a te ragion rubella?
    Nè ti comprendo ancor.

Os: (Non merta più consiglio
    il misero mio stato;
    è il più crudel periglio
    vo intrepido a sfidar.)

Fa: (Palpito a quell'aspetto!
    Gemo nel suo dolor!
    Ah! qual sarà l'oggetto
    del grave suo penar?)
    Ma che t'affanna?

Os: Non posso, Padre . . . Ah! non sai . . .

I cannot express or explain
what I feel in my heart.
Ah no! . . . There cannot be
greater torment than mine.

Heaven is serene for us,
though once adverse and haughty:
sweet and gentle love, so I hope,
will calm you.

No . . . always unfortunate . . .

Why? What sad event?

Father! Ah! I don't know . . .

Speak . . .

My evil star
always wants to oppress me.

Have you been robbed of your reason?
I do not yet understand you.

(My miserable state no longer
deserves counsel.
It is the cruellest danger
to defy your bravery.)

(I tremble at his appearance!
I groan at his grief!
Ah! What can be the object
of his deep sorrow?)
But what distresses you?

I cannot, Father . . . Ah! I do not know.

SOURCE: *Opera*, Collana di guide musicali diretta da Alberto Basso, serie prima #4 (Turin, 1974).

[18] "Assisa a piè"

De: "Assisa a piè d'un salice,
   immersa nel dolore,
   gemea trafitta Isaura
   dal più crudele amore:
   L'aura fra i rami flebile
   ne ripeteva il suon.

   "I ruscelletti limpidi
   a' caldi suoi sospiri,
   il mormorio mesceano
   de' lor diversi giri:
   L'aura fra i rami flebile

   "Salce d'amor delizia!
   Ombra pietosa appresta,
   di mie sciagure immemore,
   all'urna mia funesta;
   nè più ripeta l'aura
   de' miei lamenti il suon."

Che dissi! . . . Ah m'ingannai! . . . Non è del
canto questo il lugubre fin. M'ascolta . . .

Oh Dio!
Qual mai strepito è questo!
Qual presagio funesto!

Em: Non paventar; rimira:
   Impetuoso vento è quel, che spira.

De: Io credeva che alcuno . . .
   Oh come il Cielo
   s'unisce a' miei lamenti! . . .
   Ascolta il fin de' dolorosi accenti.

   "Ma stanca alfin di spargere
   mesti sospiri e pianto,
   morì l'afflitta vergine
   ahi! di quel salce accanto."
   Morì . . . che duol! l'ingrato . . .

Oimè . . . ma il pianto proseguir non mi fa.
Parti, ricevi da' labbri dell'amica il bacio estremo.

Em: Ah che dici! Ubbidisco . . . oh come tremo!

De: Deh calma, o Ciel, nel sonno
   per poco le mie pene,
   fa', che l'amato bene
   mi venga a consolar.
   Se poi son vani i prieghi,
   di mia breve urna in seno
   di pianto venga almeno
   il cenere a bagnar.

[19] Ah, quel giorno ognor rammento

Ah, quel giorno ognor rammento
di mia gloria e di contento,
che fra barbari potei
vita e onore a lei serbar.

L'involava in queste braccia
al suo vile rapitore;
io sentia contro il mio core
il suo core palpitar.

Schiuse il ciglio . . . mi guardò . . .
mi sorrise . . . e palpitò.

"Seated at the foot of a willow,
sunk in grief
moans Isaura, wounded
by cruellest love:
The breeze through the bending branches
repeats her sounds.

"The crystal streams add
to the warmth of her sighs
the murmur
of their various circlings:
the breeze though the bending branches

"Willow, delight of love!
Prepare a merciful shade,
heedless of my misfortunes
for my dark tomb;
and let the freeze no longer repeat
the sound of my laments."

What did I say! . . . Ah, I was mistaken! . . . This is not the
sad ending of this song. Listen . . .

O God!
What a sound that was!
What a dark omen!

Don't be afraid; look,
it is the wild wind blowing.

I thought that someone . . .
Oh, how heaven
joins in my laments! . . .
Hear the end of my sad tale.

"But weary at last of pouring out
sorrowful sighs and tears,
the tormented virgin died—
ah!—beside the willow."
She died . . . how sad! Ungrateful man . . .

Alas! . . . But tears won't let me go on. Go, receive from
your friend's lips her last kiss.

Ah! What are you saying? I obey . . . Oh, how I tremble!

O heaven, in sleep calm
my anguish for a while,
make my beloved
come to console me.
But if my prayers are in vain,
into the depths of my little tomb
let him at least come with tears
to bathe the ashes.

Ah, I shall always remember that day
of my glory and happiness,
when, from among barbarians, I was able
to preserve her life and honor.

I grabbed her up in these arms
from her vile abductor;
I felt against my heart
Her heart beating.

She opened her eyes . . . looked at me . . .
smiled at me . . . and trembled.

Oh! come da quel dì	Oh! Since that day how
tutto per me cangiò;	everything has changed for me.
quel guardo mi rapì,	That look ravished me—
sì, quest'anima avvampò.	yes, this heart was set ablaze.
Il cielo per me s'aprì,	Heaven opened before me,
amore si m'animò.	love brought me back to life.
D'Azema, di quel dì,	Azema and that day
no, scordarmi io mai saprò.	I shall never be able to forget.

SOURCE: *Semiramis: A Tragico-Dramatic Opera* (New York: Houel and Macoy, 1845).

Concerning the text of Cinti-Damoreau's embellishments, see the Critical Notes for this aria.

[20] Du séjour de la lumière

Du séjour de la lumière	From the abode of light
Daigne, hélas, ma tendre mère	deign, alas, my tender mother,
Accueillir ma prière	to receive my prayer
Et veiller sur mon destin.	and to watch over my fate.
Mais après un long orage,	But after a long tumult my homeland,
A l'abri de l'esclavage,	rescued from slavery
Ma patrie, ô doux présage,	(O sweet omen),
Reverra ses plus beaux jours.	shall again see its happiest days.

[21] Di tanti palpiti

Oh patria! dolce, e ingrata patria! alfine a te ritorno! Io ti saluto, o cara terra degli avi miei: ti bacio.

O homeland, sweet and ungrateful homeland, finally I return to you! I salute you, O beloved soil of my ancestors; I kiss you.

È questo per me giorno sereno:
comincia il cor a respirarmi in seno.
Amenaide!

How joyful is this day for me;
my heart begins to beat in my breast.
Amenaide!

O mio pensier soave, solo de' miei sospir, de' voti miei celeste oggetto, io venni alfin: io voglio, sfidando il mio destino, qualunque sia, meritarti, o perir, anima mia.

O tender thought, heavenly object of my sighs and prayers, finally I return: defying my destiny, whatever it be, I long to be worthy of you, my soul, or to die.

Tu che accendi questo core,	You who set fire to this heart,
tu che desti il valor mio,	you who awoke my valor,
alma gloria, dolce amore,	glorious soul, sweet love,
secondate il bel desio,	favor a great desire,
cada un empio traditore,	hurl down an impious traitor,
coronate la mia fé.	crown my steadfast faith.
Di tanti palpiti,	For so many throbbings,
di tante pene,	for so many sorrows,
da te mio bene,	from you, my love,
spero mercé.	I hope for pity.
Mi rivedrai . . .	You will see me again . . .
ti rivedrò . . .	I will see you . . .
ne' tuoi bei rai	on your sweet glances
mi pascerò.	I will feed.
Deliri, sospiri . . .	Ecstasies, sighs . . .
accenti, contenti . . .	murmurings, delights! . . .
Sarà felice, il cor mel dice,	My heart tells me that near you
il mio destino vicino a te.	my fate will be happy.

Concerning the text of Cinti-Damoreau's embellishments, see the Critical Notes for this aria.

[22] Lasciami: non t'ascolto

Tan: Lasciami: non t'ascolto:	Leave me, I will not listen to you;
sedurmi invan tu speri:	you hope in vain to tempt me.
que' sguardi lusinghieri	Save those flattering looks
serba al novello amor.	for your new love.

Ame: Odimi: e poi m'uccidi:
sì, che innocente io sono:
riprenditi il tuo dono,
se rea mi credi ancor.

Tan: Ah! come mai quell'anima
cangiò per me d'affetto!
Per chi sospiri in petto
o debole mio cor?

Ame: Ah! che fedel quest'anima
serbò il giurato affetto. . . .
Fosti tu sol l'oggetto
del tenero mio cor.

Dunque?

Tan: Addio.

Ame: Lasciarmi puoi?

Tan: Che più vuoi? . . .

Ame: Seguirti.

Tan: Trema.

Ame: E qui sfoga il tuo furore.

Both: Ah! si mora, e cessi omai
l'atro orror de' mali miei.

Hear me, then kill me—
yes, though I am innocent:
take back your gift,
if you still believe me guilty.

Ah! How could her heart
be turned against me!
For whom are you secretly longing,
O my feeble heart?

Ah! How faithfully this heart
served its sworn love. . . .
You were the only object
of my tender heart.

And now?

Goodbye.

You can leave me?

What more do you want? . . .

To follow you.

Tremble.

Then vent your hatred here [in my breast].

Ah! Let me die and end forever
the horrible agony of my woes.

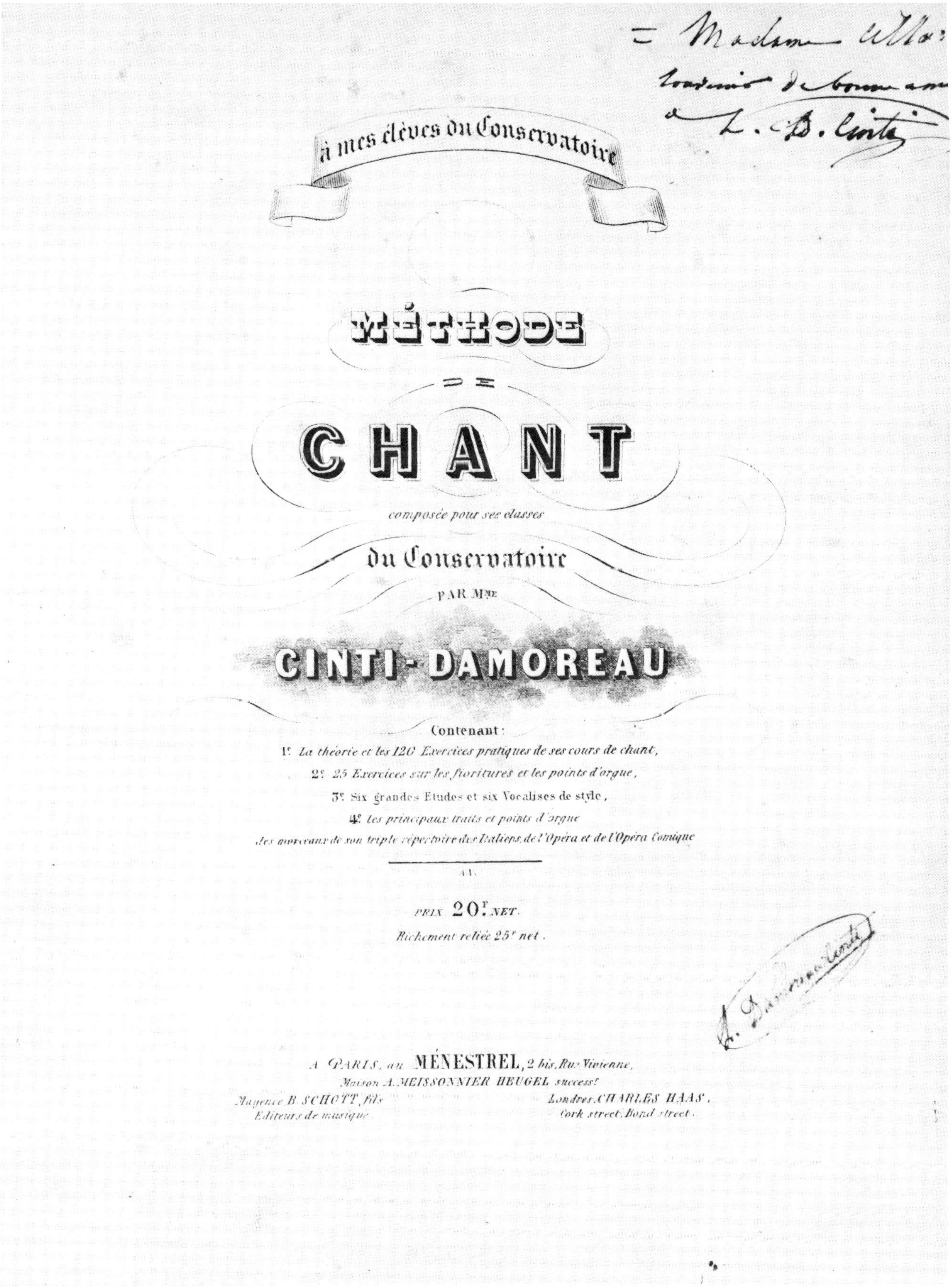

à mes élèves du Conservatoire

MÉTHODE
DE
CHANT
composée pour ses classes
du Conservatoire
PAR Mme
CINTI-DAMOREAU

Contenant:

1° La théorie et les 120 Exercices pratiques de ses cours de chant,
2° 25 Exercices sur les fioritures et les points d'orgue,
3° Six grandes Etudes et six Vocalises de style,
4° les principaux traits et points d'orgue
des morceaux de son triple répertoire des Italiens, de l'Opéra et de l'Opéra Comique

PRIX 20f NET.
Richement reliée 25f net.

A PARIS, au MÉNESTREL, 2 bis, Rue Vivienne,
Maison A. MEISSONNIER HEUGEL successr
Mayence B. SCHOTT, fils
Editeurs de musique
Londres, CHARLES HAAS,
Cork street, Bond street.

Plate 1. Laure Cinti-Damoreau, *Méthode de chant composée pour ses classes du Conservatoire par Mme Cinti-Damoreau* (Paris: Au Ménestrel, 1849), title page. Actual size: 25.5 x 33 cm. (Courtesy Lilly Library, Indiana University, Bloomington)

Plate 2. Laure Cinti-Damoreau, "Points d'orgue et variantes composées par Mme Cinti-Damoreau pour differents airs" (Lilly Library, Helm MSS, Cinti-Damoreau notebook I, undated), p. 41, showing embellishments for "Come per me sereno" from Bellini's *La sonnambula* ([3] in this edition). Actual size: 14.6 x 22.2 cm. (Courtesy Lilly Library, Indiana University, Bloomington)

Plate 3. Laure Cinti-Damoreau, untitled MS (Lilly Library, Helm MSS, Cinti-Damoreau notebook III, undated), p. 20, showing embellishments for "Comme aux jours" from Boieldieu's *La dame blanche* ([5] in this edition). Actual size: 15.2 x 23 cm. (Courtesy Lilly Library, Indiana University, Bloomington)

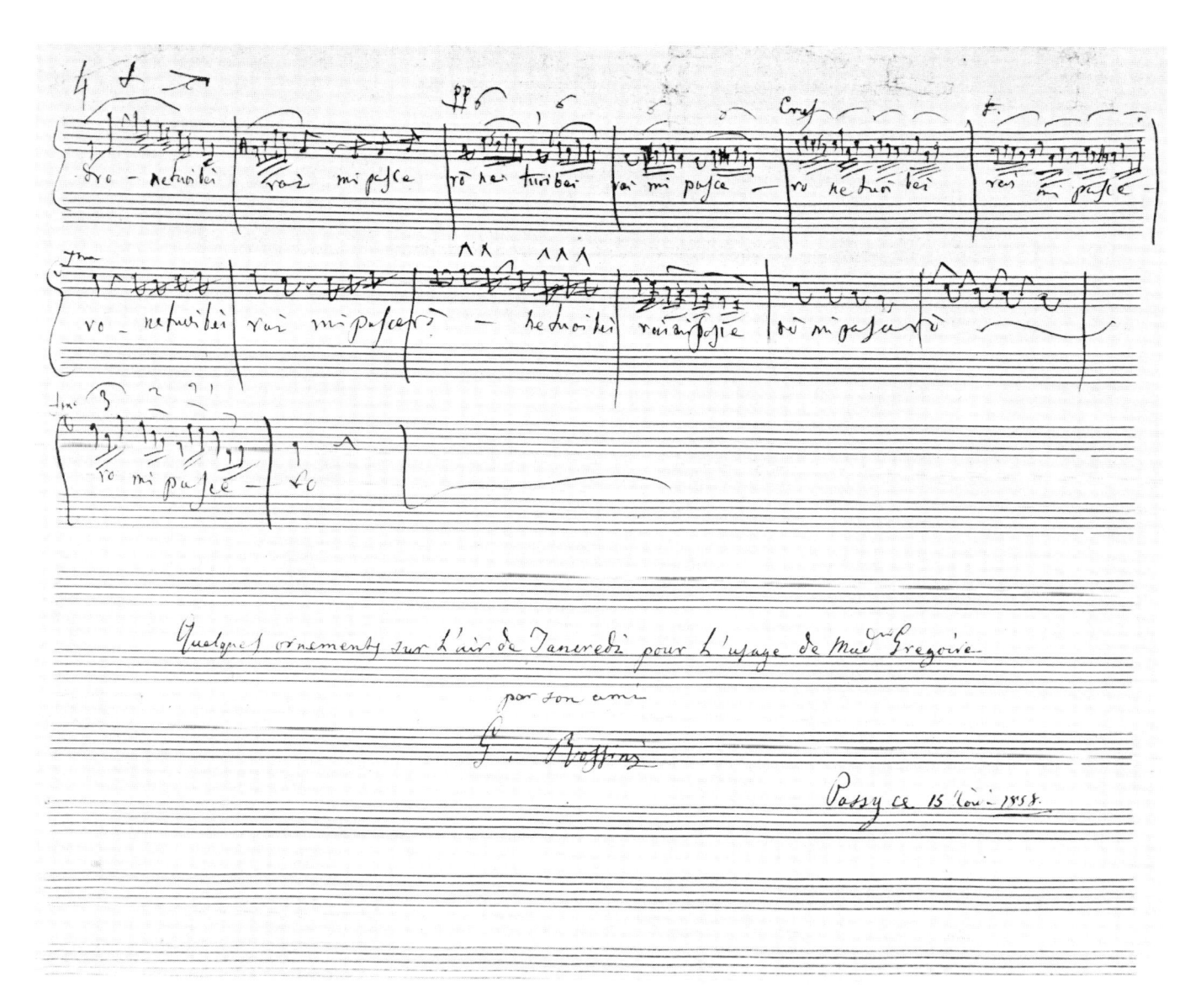

Plate 4. Gioachino Rossini, "Quelques ornements sur l'air de Tancredi pour l'usage de Mad^me Gregoire par son ami G. Rossini" (autograph dated "Passy ce 15 Août 1858," Cary Collection 177, Pierpont Morgan Library, New York), p. 3, showing embellishments for the end of "Di tanti palpiti" from *Tancredi* ([21] in this edition). Actual size: 27 x 34.5 cm. (Courtesy Pierpont Morgan Library, New York)

Plate 5. Gioachino Rossini, "... Cavatina in the Opera of Il Tancredi, Composed by Rossini, Arranged with an Accompaniment for the Piano Forte" (London: Clementi and Co., n.d. [1821–28]), p. 5, showing embellishments by an anonymous singer for "Di tanti palpiti" ([21] in this edition). (Author's collection)

[1] Ma la sola
(*Beatrice di Tenda*)

Vincenzo Bellini

Ma la so- la, ohi-mè, ohi-mè! son i- o, che pe-nar, che pe-nar per lui si ve- da? O mie genti! O suol na- ti- o! O mie genti! di chi mai vi die-di, vi die-di in pre-da? Ed io stes-sa, ed io po-tei sog-get-tar via un tal, a un tal si-gnor?

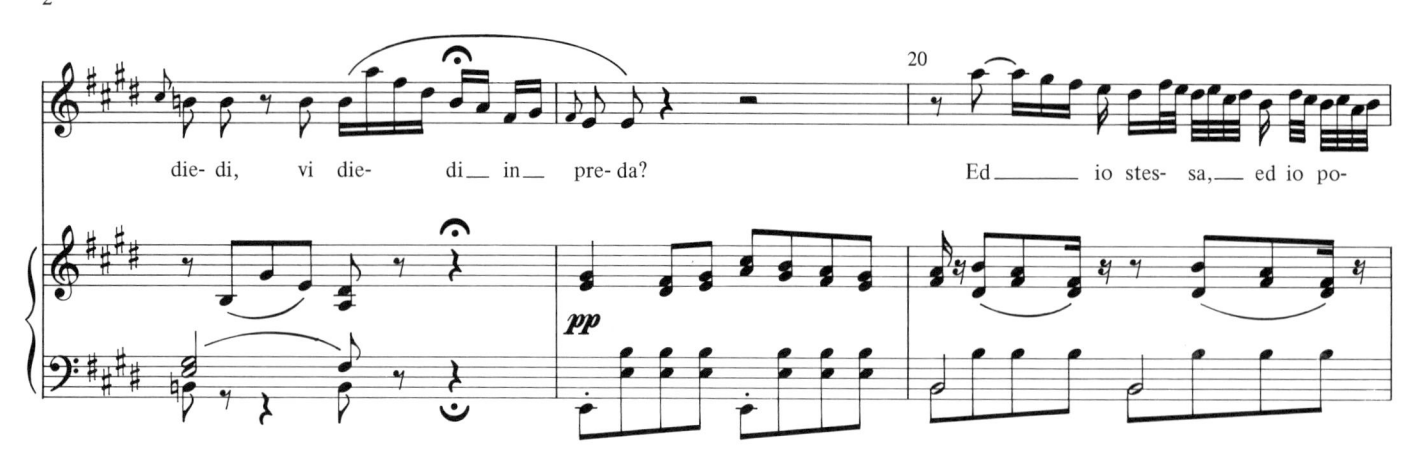

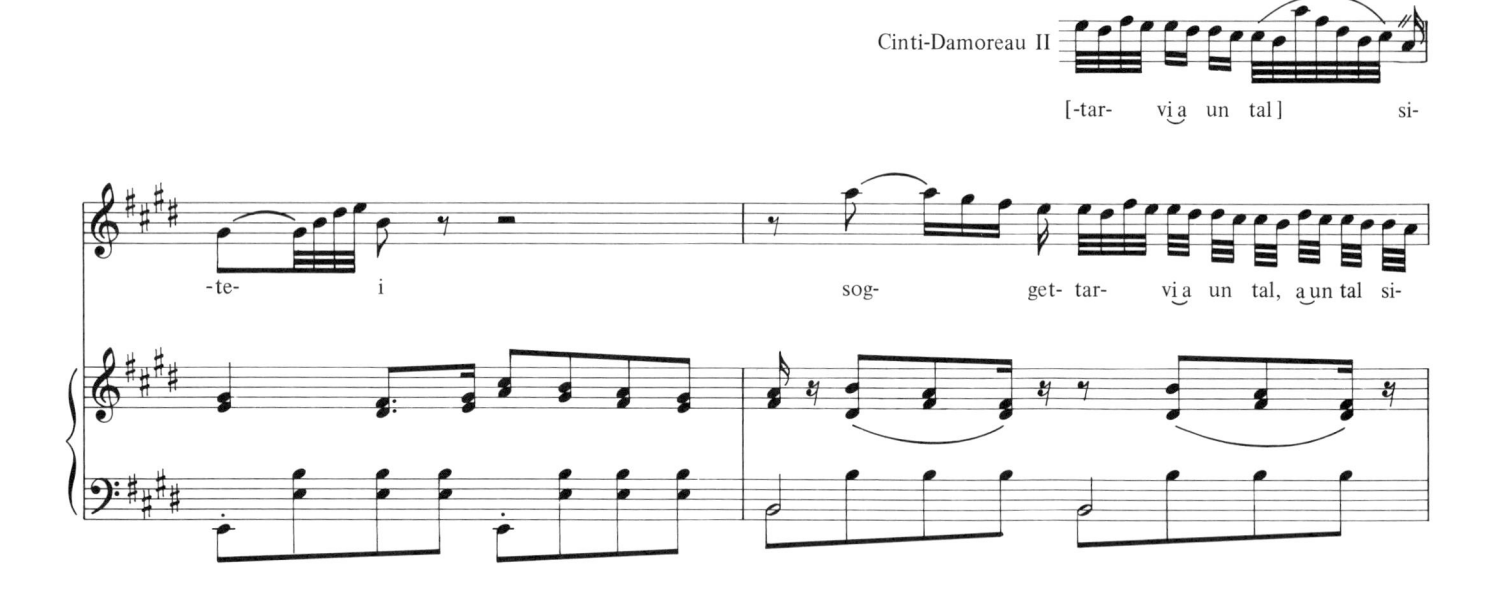

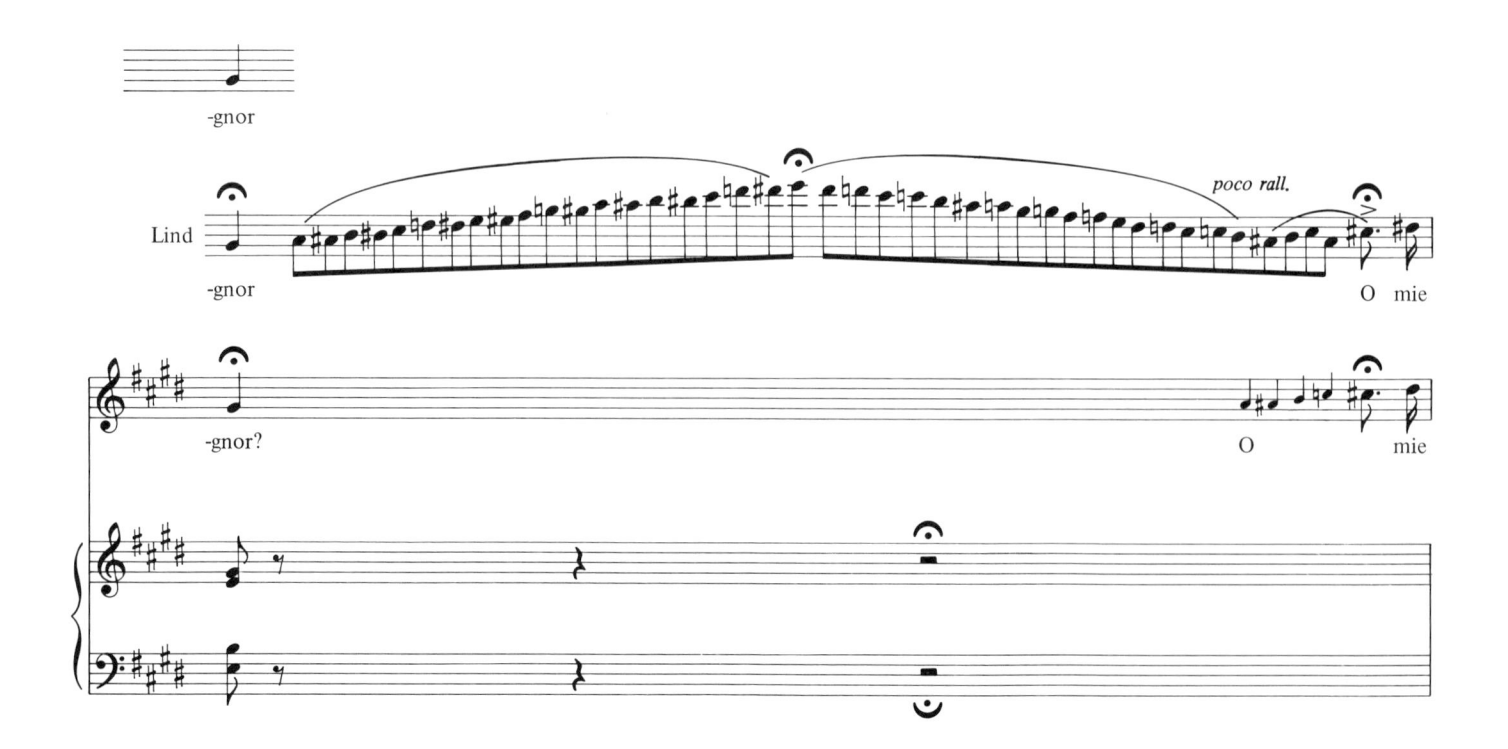

Cinti-Damoreau II: [-tar-via un tal] si-gnor

Lind: -gnor O mie

poco rall.

Cinti-Damoreau II
o suol na- ti- o
gen- ti! O suol na- ti- o! O re- gni mie- i! ed io po-
25
[-tar- vi a] tal si-
-te- i, ed io po- te- i sog- get-tar- vi a tal si-
-gnor
-te- i
30
-gnor? O re- gni mie- i! ed io po- te- i, ed io po-
[6] [6]
-te- i sog- get-tar- vi a tal si-
-te- i sog- get- tar- vi a tal si-

-gnor
Ah
Lind
Oh
p
35
-gnor? sog- get- tar- vi?
O
Lind
f
f
accel.
Cinti-
Damoreau II
mio ros- sor
Lind
rall.
p
pp
mio ros- sor!
40
mio ros- sor!
Allegro moderato

45
p cresc.
50
Ah! la
f
55
pe- na in lor piom- bò dell' a- mor che mi per- dè; i mar-
-tir do- vu- ti a me il de- stin a lor ser- bò.
60
Mu- se in
ciel spe-rar si può un sol rag- gio di pie- tà, la co-

un poco più sostenuto
65
-stan- za a noi da- rà, se la pa- ce, ne in- vo- lò, se la
pa- ce, la pa- -
70
-ce, la pa- ce ne in- vo- lò.
75
p
p
O mie gen- ti!
80
cresc.
O suol na- ti- o!

85
90
8
Cinti-Damoreau II
Ah
Lind
f
f
f
rall.
pp
sempre p
[Ah]
Ah!
Lind
pp
rall.

a tempo
Ah! la pe- na in lor piom-
Cinti-Damoreau II
[mor] che mi per-
95
Ah! la pe- na in lor piom- bò dell' a- mor che mi per-
[autre]
vu- ti a
-dè I mar- tir do- vu- ti a me
100
-dè; i mar- tir do- vu- ti a me il de-
a lor ser- bò
[può] un sol
105
-stin a lor ser- bò. Mu- se in ciel spe-rar si può un sol
rag- gio di pie- ta
un poco più sostenuto
rag- gio di pie- tà, la co- stan- za a noi da- rà, se la

110
pa- ce, ne in- vo- lô, se la pa- ce, la pa-
115
- ce, la pa- ce ne in- vo-
mosso
-lò, la co- stan- za a noi, a noi da-
120
-rà, a noi da- rà, la co- stan- za a
125

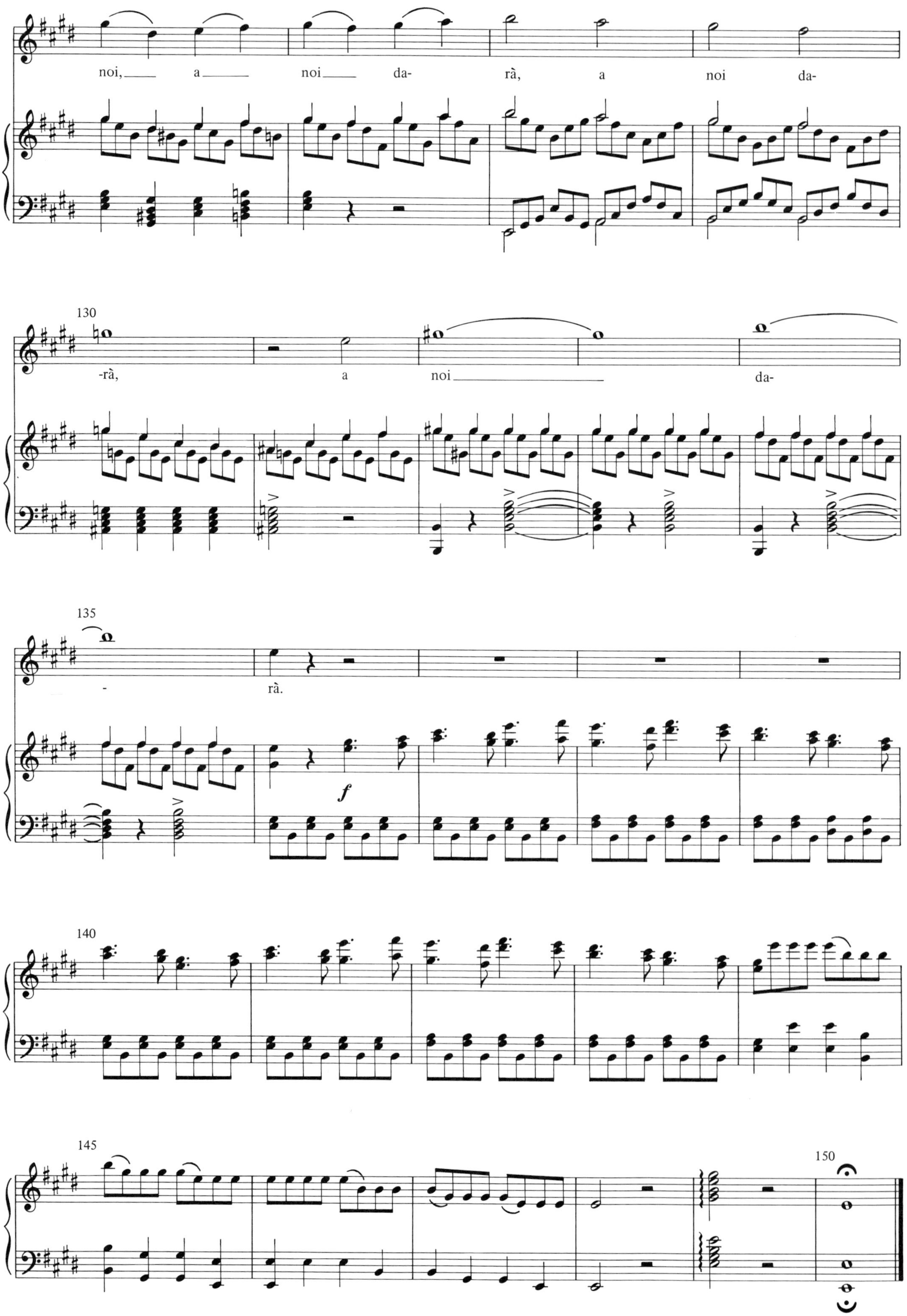
noi, a noi da- rà, a noi da-
130
-rà, a noi da-
135
- rà.
140
145
150

[2] Ah! non credea mirarti
(*La sonnambula*)

Vincenzo Bellini

* "The embellishments of Cadenze in this piece were sung in moderate time, not quickly." See Critical Notes.

so- lo, che un gior- no sol du- rò, che un gior- no
so- lo, che un gior- no sol__ du- rò,___ che un gior- no

so- lo ah! sol du- rò.
so- lo, ah,__ sol du- rò.

Pas- sa- sti al par d'a- mo- re,
Pas- sa- sti al par d'a- mo- re,

Che un gior- no, che un gior- no sol du-
che un gior- no, che un gior- no sol du-

-rò

molto espressivo

Po- tria no- vel vi- -rò. Po- tria no- vel vi-

go- re, Il pian-to, il pian-to mio re- car- ti,
go- re il pian-to, il pian-to mio re- car- ti,

Ma rav- vi- var l'a- mo- re il pian- to
ma rav- vi- var l'a- mo- re il_pian- to

Cadenza

mi- o ah no, no non più ah non cre- de- a ah non cre-
mio, ah, no, no, non può! Ah! non cre- de- a, ah! non cre-

-a. Pas- sa- sti al par, al par d'a- mo- re che un gior- no sol du- rò, che un gior- no sol du-
abbandonandosi
35
-a. Pas- sa- sti al par, al par d'a- mor, che un gior- no sol du- rò, che un gior- no sol du-
colla parte
lento
-rò, che un gior- no
rall.
lento
-rò, pas- sa- sti al par d'a-
lento
Cadenza
tranquillo
accel.
sol du-
-mor, d'a-
-rò.
40
-mor.

[3] Come per me sereno
(*La sonnambula*)

Vincenzo Bellini

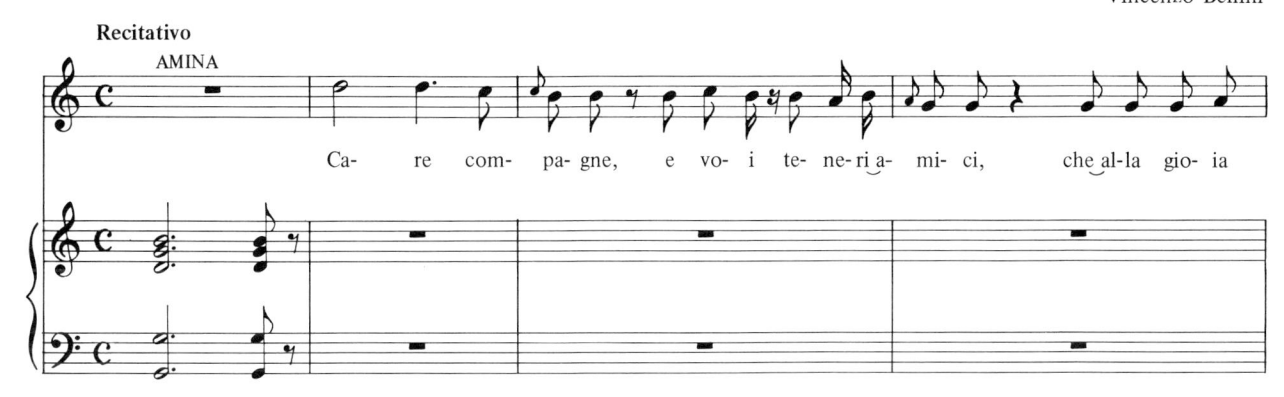

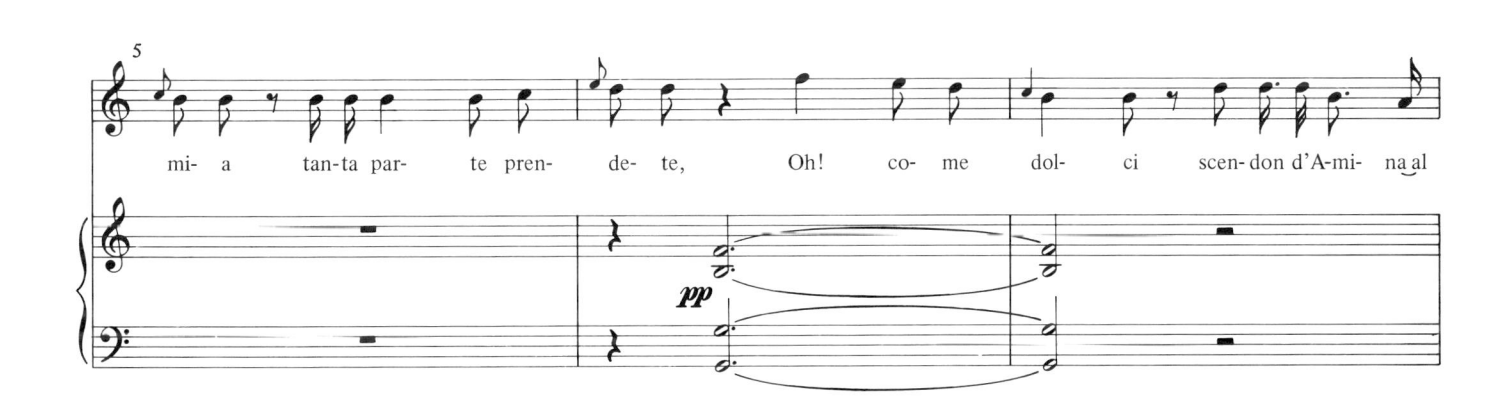

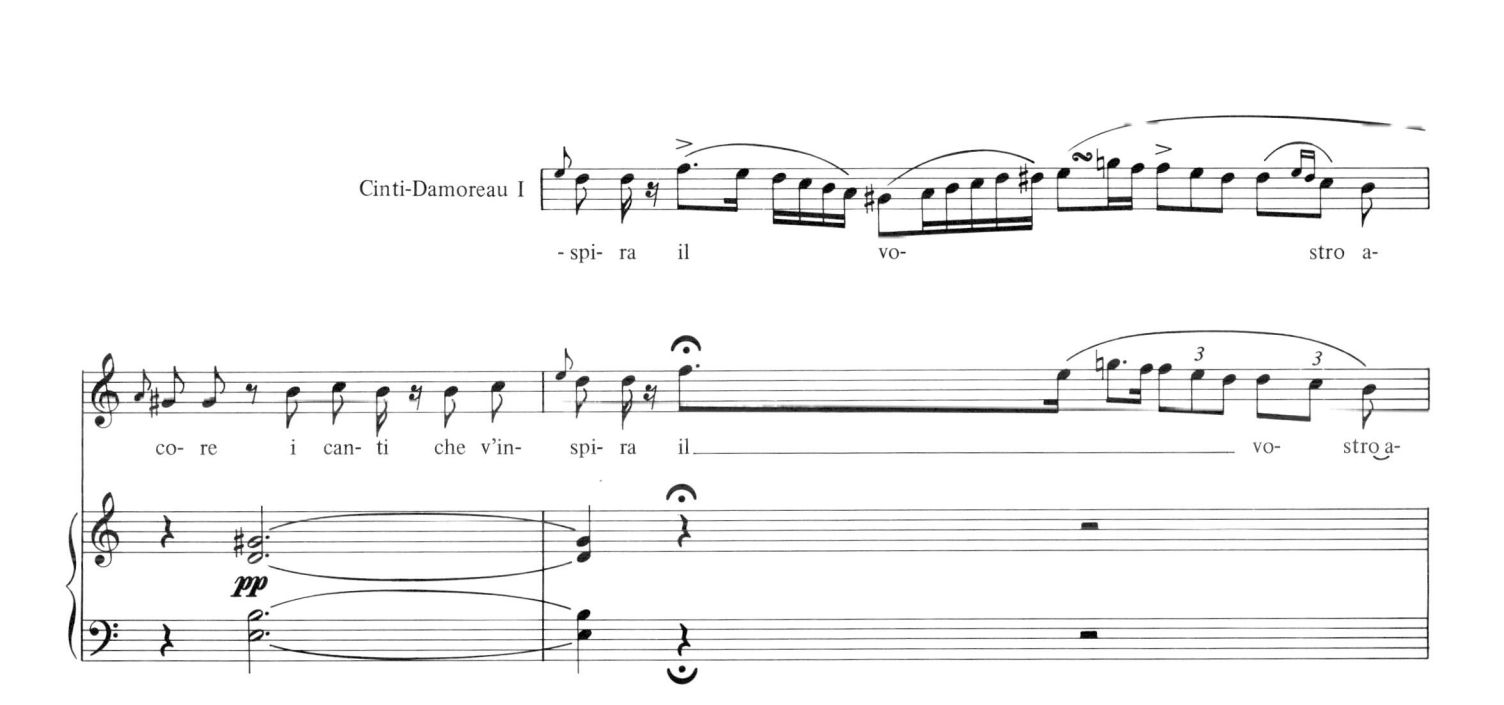

Recitativo

AMINA: Care compagne, e voi teneri amici, che alla gioia mia tanta parte prendete, Oh! come dolci scendon d'Amina al core i canti che v'inspira il vostro a-

Cinti-Damoreau I: spira il vostro a-

-mo- re

-mo- re!

Andante

Recitativo

A te, di- let- ta, te- ne- ra ma- dre, che a sì lie- to gior- no me or- fa- nel- la ser- ba- sti, a te fa-

Cinti-Damoreau 1

-spres- so dol- ce pian- to di -vel- li que- sto, dal cor più che dal ci- glio e- spres- so dol- ce pian- to di

gio- ja
Andante mosso
gio- ia, dol- ce pian- to di gio- ia, e que- sto am- ples- so.
ff
pp
30
(con tenero contento)
Com- pa-gne . . . te- ne- ri a-
p
35
-mi- ci . . . ah ma-dre, ah qual glo- ia!
40
Cantabile sostenuto assai
Co- me per me se- re- no og- gi ri- na- que il
p
3

45
dì! Co- me il ter-ren fio- rì, co- me fio-
colla parte
Cinti-Damoreau I
più bel- lo e a- me- no
a piacere
-rì più bel- lo, più bel- lo e a- me- no! Ma- i, mai di più lie- to a-
in tempo
bril-
50
-spet- to na-tu- ra, na- tu- ra non, non bril-

bis
non bril- lo
-lò non bril- lo
-lò, non bril- lò: a- mor, a- mor la co- lo- rò, a-
colla parte
-del mi- o del mi- o di-
55
-mor, del mi- o, del mi- o di-
-let- to
a-mor la co-lo- ro a-
-let- to, a- mor, a-mor la co-lo- rò, a-
in tempo

Cinti-Damoreau, Méthode
a- mo- re la
p
Cinti-Damoreau I
-mor a- mor del
59
-mor, a- mor,
cresc. rallent:
co- lo- rò
mio di- let- to
60
del mio di- let- to.
Marchisio
59
a- mor del mio di- let- to a-
-mor ah accel. a- mor la co- lo- rò
60
Marchisio
59
pp
la co- lo- rò a-
-mor a- mor
60
Marchisio
59
del mi- o di- let- to a- mor, a-
-mor la co- lo- rò la co- lo- rò a- mor
60

So- vra il sen la___ man mi po- sa; pal- pi-

Cinti-Damoreau I
non ha
-tar, bal- zar, bal- zar lo sen- ti; e- gli è il cor che i suoi con- ten- ti non ha
85
for- za a so- ste- ner
for- za a so- ste- ner. Ah! non ha for-
90
ff
pp
rall.
a so- ste- ner a so- ste- ner ah no ah
- za a so- ste- ner, a so- ste- ner, ah! no, ah!
no ah no ah no
no, ah! no, ah! no, a so-
95
a piacere
colla parte

100
-ste- ner. So- vra il sen la man mi
Cinti-Damoreau I
pal- pi- tar bal- zar lo sen- ti egli è il
po- sa; pal- pi- tar, bal- zar, bal- zar lo sen- ti; e- gli è il
bis
so- ste-
so- ste
cor che i suoi con- ten- ti
105
di forza
cor che i suo- i con- ten- ti non ha for- za a so- ste-

-ner
-ner
110
-ner.
Ca-
ri a-
più vivo
-mi-
ci . . .
a-
ma-
ta
115
ma-
dre . . .
Cinti-Damoreau I
ah
rall.
120
Ah!

So- vra il sen la man mi po- sa pal- pi-
So- vra il sen la man mi po- sa; pal- pi-
a tempo
pp
-tar bal zar lo sen- ti egli è il cor che i suoi con-
pp
125
-tar bal- zar, bal- zar lo sen- ti; e- gli è il cor che i suoi con-
-ten- ti
130
-ten- ti non ha for- za a so- ste- ner. Ah! non ha
ff
pp
for- za a so- ste- ner, a so- ste-

135
a piacere
-ner, ah! no, ah! no, ah! no, ah! no, a so-
colla parte
Marchisio
so- vra il sen la man mi
-ste- ner.
140
So- vra il sen la man mi
po- sa pal- pi- tar bal-zar lo sen- ti egli è il
po- sa; pal- pi- tar, bal- zar, bal- zar lo sen- ti; e- gli è il
Cinti-Damoreau I
for- za a so- ste-
cor che i suoi con- ten- ti non ha [for- za a so- ste-
145
di forza
cor che i suo- i con- ten- ti non ha for- za a so- ste-

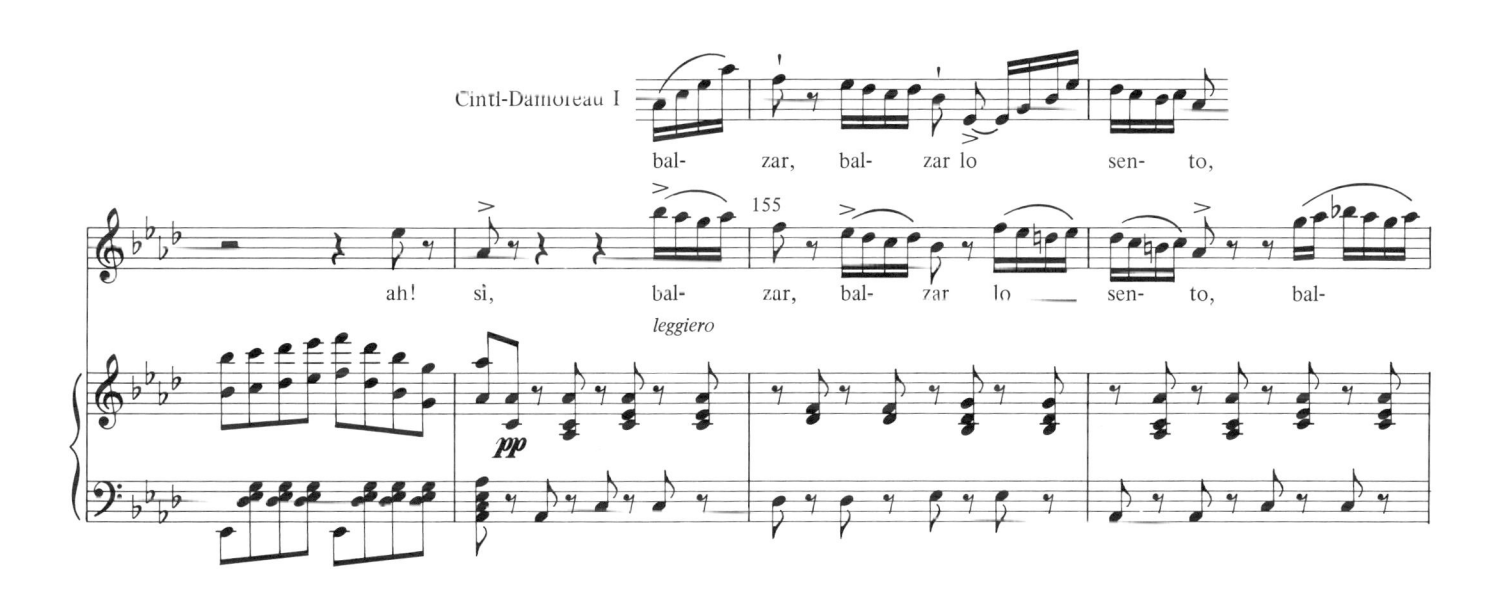

-ner

-ner.]

-ner. Ah! lo sen- to, è il mio co- re,

f più vivo ... *ff*

Cinti-Damoreau I

bal- zar, bal- zar lo sen- to, ah! sì, bal- zar, bal- zar lo sen- to, bal-

leggiero *pp*

-zar, bal- zar lo sen- to, ah sì lo sen- to bal-zar, bal- zar lo sen- to, lo sen-

p

28

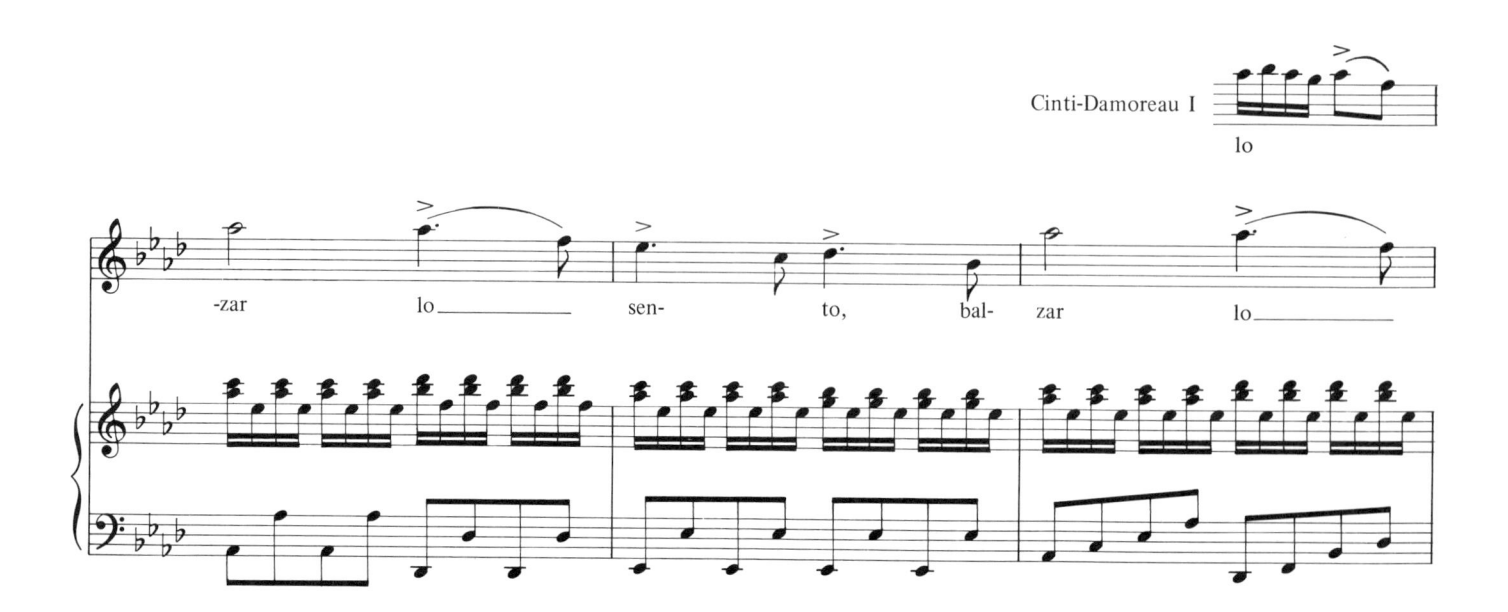

-zar -to, bal- — — *con gran forza* -zar, bal- -zar lo— sen- to, bal- zar lo—

Cinti-Damoreau I
lo

sen- to bal- zar, - -
170
sen- to, bal- zar, bal- zar, bal- zar, bal-
pour les peureuses
bal- zar
au besoin
bal- zar
-zar, bal- zar
-zar, bal- zar.
175
180

[4] De tous les pays
(*Le calife de Bagdad*)

François-Adrien Boieldieu

KESIE *Récit.*
De tous les pa-ys, pour vous plai-re, Je sau-rai pren-dre, tour à

Cinti-Damoreau I
tour, Les goûts et le ca-rac-tè-re à Fran-çai-se vive et lé-gè-re vou-lez-vous con-sa-crer vos soins et vo-tre a-

-gè-re, Vou-ez-vous con-sa-crer vos soins et vo- tre a-

-mour

D'u- ne flam- me si bel- le, Pour vous pay-er le prix, Je fi- dè- le je vous se- rai fi- dè- le vous se- rai fi- dè- le, je vous se- rai fi- dè- le...

Allegro

Com- me on l'est à Pa- ris, com- me on l'est à Pa- ris, com- me on à Pa- ris com- me on l'est à Pa- ris l'est à Pa- ris, com- me on l'est à Pa- ris.

32

Du chant i-ta-li-en si vous ê- tes é- -pris, Du ton le plus lamentable, Je vous peindrai mon ardeur et l'excès de la douleur qui loin de

33

50
55
Je vous at- tends, dans l'om- bre de la
nuit;
60
Loin des ja- loux, nous
très doux
je vous at-
nous ver- rons sans bruit.
65
Je vous at- tends,
je vous at-

-tends dans l'ombre de la nuit

-tends, dans l'ombre de la nuit;

loin des jaloux nous nous verrons sans bruit je vous at-

Loin des jaloux, nous nous verrons sans bruit. Je vous at-

-tends dans l'ombre de la nuit je vous attends ah!

con delicatezza

-tends, dans l'ombre de la nuit, je vous attends,

je vous attends

Allegro vivace

je vous attends.

Faudra-t'il imiter la plaintive Écossaise? Sur le sommet des monts, je ferai, nuit et jour, Répéter aux échos tendres soupirs d'amour, Répéter aux échos tendres soupirs d'amour. A mon époux, pour peu que l'Allemande plaise,

110
115
Com-me elle, on me ver- ra val- ser,
Tour-ner, pas- ser et
120
re- pas- ser.
légèrement
123
130
Com-me elle, on me ver-

135
-ra val- ser, Tour- ner, pas- ser et re- pas- ser.
140
Com-me elle, on me ver- ra val- ser, Tour- ner, pas- ser et
145
re- pas- ser. Si pour com- pa- gne en- fin,
plus animé
f
An- glai- se
150
vous vou- lez une An- glai- se,
p

Mouvement de l'Anglaise

très légèrement

Vous ver-rez qu'ou-bli- ant Par- fois leur in- do- len- ce, Il rè- gne dans leur dan- se Un ai- ma-ble en-jou- ment.

Vous ver- rez, qu'ou- bli- ant Par- fois leur in- do- len- ce, Il rè- gne dans leur dan- se Un ai- ma- ble en- jou- ment. Voi- là par quelle heu- reu- se a- dres- se, Fi- xant l'ob- jet de ma ten- dres- se, ten- dres- se, Mon é-

-poux, suivant mes désirs, Chaque jour, sans être infidèle, Auprès d'une femme nouvelle goûtera de nouveaux plaisirs -velle, Goûtera de nouveaux plaisirs, goûtera de nouveaux plaisirs, goûtera de nou-

-veaux plai- sirs

-veaux plai- sirs. Mon é- poux, sui- vant mes dé-cha- que jour sans ê- tre in- fi- dè- le

-sirs, Cha- que jour, sans ê- tre in- fi- dè- le, au- près d'une fem- me nou- vel- le goû- te-

Au- près d'u- ne fem- me nou- vel- le, Goû- te-ra de nou- veaux plai- sirs goû- te- ra de nou-

-ra de nou- veaux plai- sirs, goû- te- ra de nou-

-veaux plai- sirs gou- te- ra de nou- veaux plai- -veaux plai- sirs, goû- te- ra de nou- veaux plai- -sirs de nou- veaux plai- sirs de nou- -sirs, de nou- veaux plai- sirs, de nou- -veaux plai- sirs. -veaux plai- sirs.

[5] Comme aux jours
(*La dame blanche*)

François-Adrien Boieldieu

Andantino affettuoso
-fin je vous re-vois, je vous re-vois, sé- jour de mon en-
p
25
-fan- ce. Pour mon coeur quel- le jou- is- san- ce, pour mon coeur quel- le jou- is-
pp
30
san- ce. Et vous, et vous, mes no- bles pro- tec-
ff p ff p ff
dolce
35
-teurs, Du haut des cieux, qui sont vo- tre par-
p
40
-ta- ge, Vous n'a- vez pas per- mis que ce bel hé-ri- ta- ge Re- tom-
ff fp fz

Cinti-Damoreau III

-bât dans les mains d'in- di- gnes ra- vis- seurs. Je vous re-vois, je vous re-vois, sé- jour de mon en- fan- ce. Je vous re- vois, je vous re- vois, sé- jour de mon en- fan- ce. Et vous, et vous, mes no- bles pro- tec- teurs, ô vous, ô vous, mes no- bles pro- tec-

Allegretto
-teurs.
Com-me aux
jours de mon jeu- ne â- ge, Dai- gnez en- cor, dai- gnez gui-der mes pas. Com-me aux
jours de mon jeu- ne â- ge, Veil- lez sur moi, ne m'a- ban-don- nez pas.
En re- voy- ant ce no- ble a- si- le
De mon bon- heur, je me sou-
pp
fp

-viens Que de fois, que de fois ce sé--jour tran- quil- le A re- dit le nom de Ju--lien, a re- dit le nom de Ju- lien, Ju- lien, Ju- lien. L'é- cho fi- dè- le, l'é- cho fi- dè- le ne l'a point ou- bli- é, Il me rap- pelle, il me rap-

-pel- le
jeux nos jeux no- tre a- mi- tié
6
6
100
-pel- le nos jeux, nos jeux, no- tre a- mi- tié. En voy-
bis
[-heur,] de mon bon-
[-heur, de
6
-ant ce no- ble a- si- le De mon bon-heur, de mon bon-
ff
p
pp
heur je me sou- viens
mon bon- heur,] je me sou- viens
105
-heur, je me sou- viens.
p

Ah
Ah!
ad libitum
a tempo
Com-me aux
â- ge
-cor gui- der mes pas
110
rall.
a tempo
jours de mon jeu- ne â- ge, Dai- gnez en- cor, dai- gnez gui- der mes pas. Com-me aux
pp
jours de mon jeu- ne â- ge, Veil- lez sur moi, ne m'a- ban- don- nez
pp
115 più animato
pas. En voy- ant ce no- ble a- si- le De mon bon-heur, je me sou-
sfz
p

51

-viens, de mon bon-heur, je me sou- viens,_____ Tout me rap--pel- le,____ tout me rap- pel- le Ju-lien, Ju-lien! L'é-cho fi--dè- le ne l'a pas ou- bli- é, l'é-cho fi- dè- le ne l'a pas ou- bli--é, Il me rap- pel- le___ no-tre__ jeu- ne a-mi-

l'é- cho fi- dè- le ne l'a pas ou-bli-
135
-tié, Ju-lien, Ju-lien! L'é-cho fi- dè- le ne l'a pas ou- bli-
pp
sfz
p
-é l'é- cho fi- dè- le ne l'a pas ou- bli- é il me rap-
animato
-é, l'é-cho fi- dè- le ne l'a pas ou- bli- é, Il me rap-
sfz
p
-pel- le
140
-pel- le no- tre jeu- ne a- mi- tié, il me rap-
sfz
p
-pel- le, il me rap- pel- le nos jeux, no- tre jeu- ne a- mi-
sfz
p
fp
fp
fp
fp

145
il me rap- pel- le il me rap- pel- le nos
-tié, il me rap- pel- le, il me rap- pel- le nos
sfz p sfz p fp fp
autre
-pel- le nos
-pel- le nos
jeux
150
jeux, notre jeu- ne a mi- tié, tout me rap- pel- le nos
fp fp ff
jeux
jeux no- tre a- mi- tié
jeux, no- tre a- mi- tié.
ff ff
155

[6] Non, je ne veux pas chanter
(*Le billet de loterie*)

Nicolas Isouard

Cinti-Damoreau I: que je vous

-ter, je ne veux pas chanter. Que vou-lez- vous que je vous chan- te? Est-ce un air sim- ple et gra-ci-eux, Qui vous cap- ti- ve et vous en-chan- te qui vous cap-ti- ve et vous en- chan- te, qui vous cap-ti- ve et vous en- chan- te Par des ac- cents mé- lo- di-

Andante à volonté

Andante sostenuto

rallent.

[3]
que vou- lez- vous que je vous chan- te est- ce un air
-eux? Que vou- lez- vous que je vous chan- te? Est- ce un air
sim- ple et gra- ci- eux qui vous cap- ti- ve et vous en-
40
sim- ple et gra- ci- eux, Qui vous cap- ti- ve et vous en-
ritar.
-chan- te par des ac- cens mé- lo- di-
lento
-chan- te Par des ac- cents mé- lo- di-
-eux
45
-eux? Chan- te-
dolce
simile

-rai- je un ron-deau fa- ci- le Qui fas-se naî- tre la___ gaie- té? Et par-

-tout com-me un vau- de- vil- le Soit re- te- nu, soit ré- pé- té?

Chan- te- rai- je un ron-deau___ fa- ci- le Qui par-

-tout com-me un vau- de vil le Soit re- te- nu, soit ré- pé- té, soit re-

-nu, soit ré- pé- té? Mais non! non!

cresc. *f*

Tempo 1°

Non, je ne veux pas chanter. Non, non, non, non, non, non! Vous pouvez bien m'écouter, vous pouvez bien m'écouter. Mais non, non, non, non, non, non, non, je ne veux pas chanter. Non, non, non, non, non, non, je ne veux pas chanter, je ne veux pas chanter!

Romance. Andantino

Au temps passé, dans plain-

-ti- ve ro- man- ce On sou- pi- rait ten- dres ac- cents d'a- -mour. Au temps pré- -sent, pour cal- mer sa souf- fran- ce pour char- mer sa souf- fran- ce, L'a- mant re- dit les chants du trou- ba- dour, l'a- mant re- dit les chants du trou- ba-

l'a- mant re- dit les chants du trou-ba- dour
-dour, l'a- mant re- dit les chants du trou-ba- dour.

Allegro maestoso

Mais non, tout me le per-su- a- de, Et je le vois bien à vos yeux, et la rou-

Et la ca- den- ce et la rou-

-la- de sont ce que vous ai- mez le
con grazia
130
-la- de Sont ce que vous ai- mez le
rf p
mieux
mieux, la ca- den- ce et
f
p
rf p
la rou- la- de
135
la rou- la- de Sont con grazia ce que
rall.
rf p
fp
vous ai- mez le mieux
a tempo
140
vous ai- mez le mieux, sont ce que vous ai- mez le
fp
fp
fp

mieux. Par mal- heur___ j'ai peu de sci- en- ce Sur la rou-

-la- de et la___ ca- den- ce, sur la rou- la-

bis
155
cresc.
Cinti-Damoreau I
de, par mal-
Cinti-Damoreau, Méthode
rallent.
la rou- la-
de par mal-
de. Par mal-
Méthode
hour
Cinti-Damoreau I
our la rou la de et la ca
160
-heur j'ai peu de sci- en- ce Sur la rou- la- de et la ca-

-den- ce, sur la rou- la-

-den- ce, sur la rou- la-

[de, la rou- la-] de
-de et la ca-

-den-

175
Cinti-Damoreau I
légèrem[t]
[ce.] non, non, non, non, non, non, [non,]
Cinti-Damoreau, Méthode
[ce.] mais non non non non non non
180
ce.
Méthode
non je ne veux pas chan- ter
Più allegro
Non, je ne veux pas chan- ter. Non, non, non, non, non, non! Vous pou-vez
Cinti-Damoreau I
vous pou-vez bien m'é- cou- ter, ah! non, non, non, non, non,
185
bien m'é- cou- ter, vous pou-vez bien m'é- cou- ter. Mais non, non, non, non, non, non,
avec finesse
fp
f

190
non, je ne veux pas chan- ter. Non, non, non, non, non, non, je ne veux
195
pas chan- ter, je ne veux pas chan- ter, je ne veux pas chan-
[autre]
[pas chan-
Cinti-Damoreau I
pas chan-
-ter, je ne veux pas chan-
-ter]
-ter.
200
-ter.

[7] En vain j'espère
(*Robert le diable*)

Giacomo Meyerbeer

68

Ten- dre pen- sé- e S'est é- clip- -sé- e Comme un beau jour, ten-dre pen- sé- e s'est é-clip-

Cinti-Damoreau III

-sé- e com- me un beau -sé- e com- me un beau

jour [Ah!]

jour. Ah!

En vain j'es-pè-re Un sort pros-pè-re; Dou-ce chi--mè-re, Rê-ves d'a-mour, A-vez fui sans re- tour, a- vez fui *piqué* sans re- tour, a- vez fui sans re- tour, sans re- tour, sans re- tour, sans re- tour

70

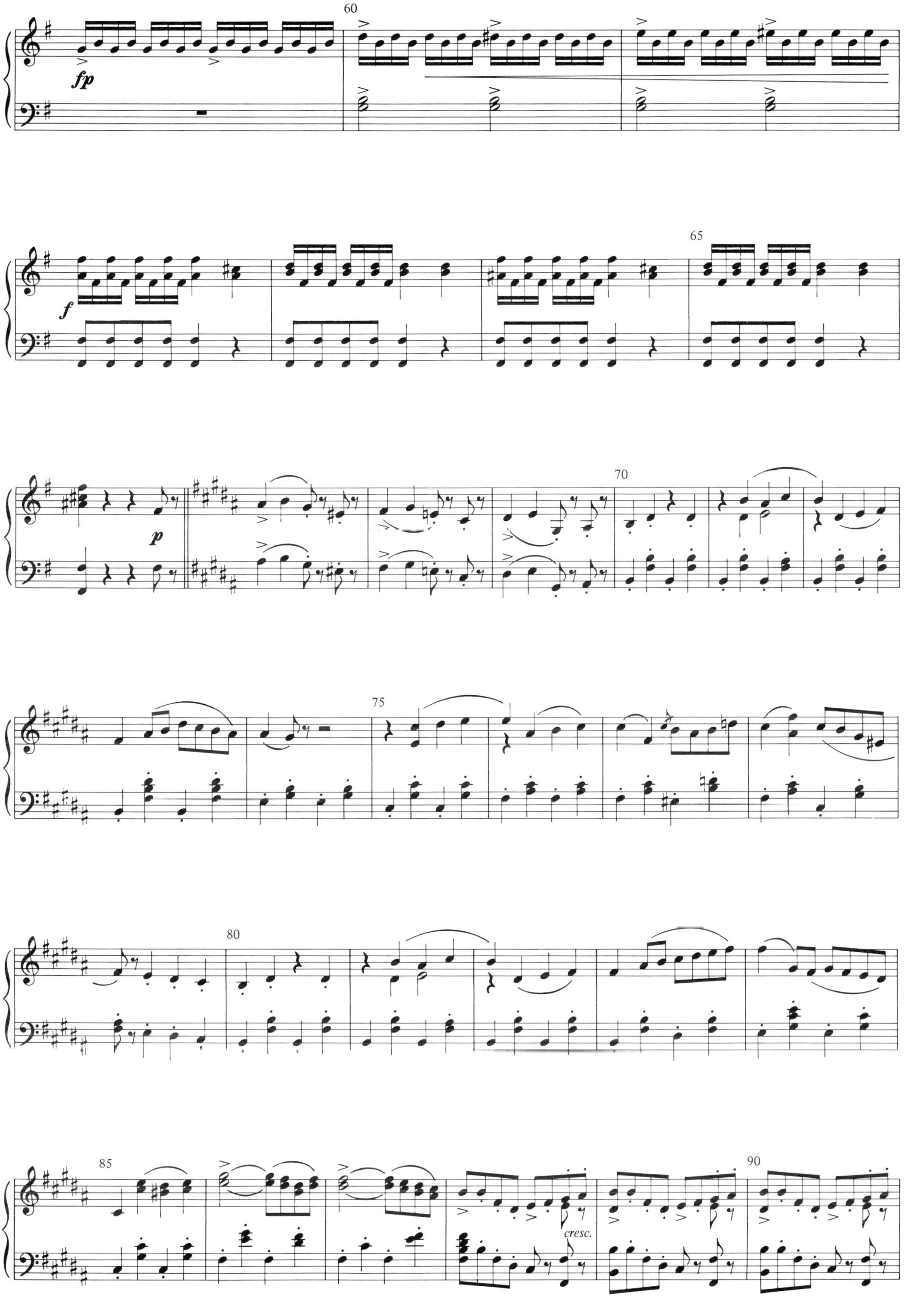
60
fp
f
65
p
70
75
80
85
cresc.
90

ALICE: Dieu! si j'o-sais... Mais les da- mes, dit- on, et les Prin- ces- ses mê- me re- çoi- vent quel- que- fois de sem- bla- bles pla- cets! Es- say- ons!

ISABELLE: Ciel! que vois- je! C'est de Ro- bert! En croi- rais- je mes yeux?

Allegretto
p et détaché
doux
léger
I- do- le de ma vi- e, Ah! viens,
Mon â- me est at- ten- dri- e! Le mal- heur qui sup- pli- e A des
droits, a des droits sur mon coeur, le mal- heur a des droits sur mon

140
dim.
rall.
coeur, le mal- heur a des droits sur mon coeur! Ah Ro- bert, ah Ro-
col canto
145
-bert! Mon bon- heur est ex- trê- me! Ro-
a tempo
pp
pp
-bert, viens, toi que j'ai- me! Ah!
staccato
150
viens, ah!
viens, ah! viens, ah! viens, toi, Ro-
155
-bert, ah! viens, ah! viens, viens,

ah!
cresc.
f
Ro- bert, ah! viens!
fp
cresc.
160
mezza voce
p
molto cresc.
mezza voce
165
molto cresc.
ff
170
doux
Ah! ah! viens, Ro-

76

Lyrics:
-bert, viens, toi que j'ai- me, ah! viens, Ro- bert, viens, toi que j'ai- me,

Cinti-Damoreau III
Ah

viens,___ ah! viens,___ ah! viens!___

[viens.]

I- do- le___ de ma vi- e, Ah!___ viens, Mon â- me est at- ten-

-dri- e! Le___ mal- heur___ qui sup- pli- e___ A des droits, a des droits sur mon

*This passage is notated with a key signature of one sharp in the source. Notes 6 and 7 of this embellishment should be sung as G-natural.

le mal- heur a des droits sur mon
dol.
dim.
190
rall.
coeur, le mal- heur a des droits sur mon coeur, le mal- heur a des droits sur mon
ff
col canto
coeur
çoeur! Ah Ro- bert, ah Ro- bert! Mon
195
pp a tempo
Cinti-Damoreau III
Ro- bert viens toi que j'ai- me.
bon- heur est ex- trê- me! Ro- bert, viens, toi que j'ai- me! Ah!
staccato
Cinti-Damoreau, Méthode
1re Var:
[viens, ah! viens, ah!
200
viens, ah! viens, ah!

1re Var:
viens, ah! viens, toi, Ro-
2e Var:
3e Var:
viens, ah! viens, toi, Ro-
-bert, ah! viens, ah!
205
-bert, ah! viens, ah!

viens,
rallent.
viens,]
rallent.
viens,
viens,
ah!
cresc.
Ro-
210
bert,
ah!
viens,
ah!
fp
doux
pp
viens,
Ro-
bert!
215
viens,
Mon a-me est at-ten-
dri-
e, mon â-me est at-ten-
dri-
e, Le mal-heur a des

Cinti-Damoreau, *Méthode*

1re Var: coeur ah

2e Var: coeur ah

3e Var: coeur ah!

4e Var: coeur ah

5e Var: coeur ah

droits____ sur mon coeur!____ Mon bon- heur est ex-

viens ah viens ah

viens viens ah

viens ah! viens

viens viens

viens ah!

-trê- me, mon bon- heur est ex- trê- me! Ah! viens, toi que j'ai- me, *viens,* ... ah! viens, oui, mon bon-heur est ex-trê-me! Ro-bert, toi que j'ai-me! Ah!

Cinti-Damoreau, *Méthode*
ah!
autre
ah!
viens,
(Méthode)
ah viens
(autre)
ah viens
ah!
viens!
ff
235

[8] Che soave zeffiretto
(Le nozze di Figaro)

Wolfgang Amadeus Mozart

sot-to i pi- ni?
sot- to i pi- ni del bo- schet- to, sot- to i
sot-to i pi- ni . . . del bo- schet-to . . .
pi- ni del bo- schet- to, ei già il
Cer-to, cer- to il ca- pi- rà, cer- to, cer- to il
re- sto ca- pi- rà, ei già il re- sto
ca- pi- rà. Che so- a- ve zef- fi-
ca- pi- rà. Can-zo-net- ta sull' a- ria.

85

rà
il ca- pi- rà
rà, il ca- pi- rà, il ca- pi-
il ca- pi- rà, il ca- pi- rà, il ca- pi-
60
Cinti-Damoreau VI
rit.
-rà il ca- pi- rà il ca- pi-
-rà il ca- pi- rà il ca- pi-
-rà, il ca- pi-
-rà, il ca- pi-
rà.
rà.
65

[9] Voi che sapete
(*Le nozze di Figaro*)

Wolfgang Amadeus Mozart

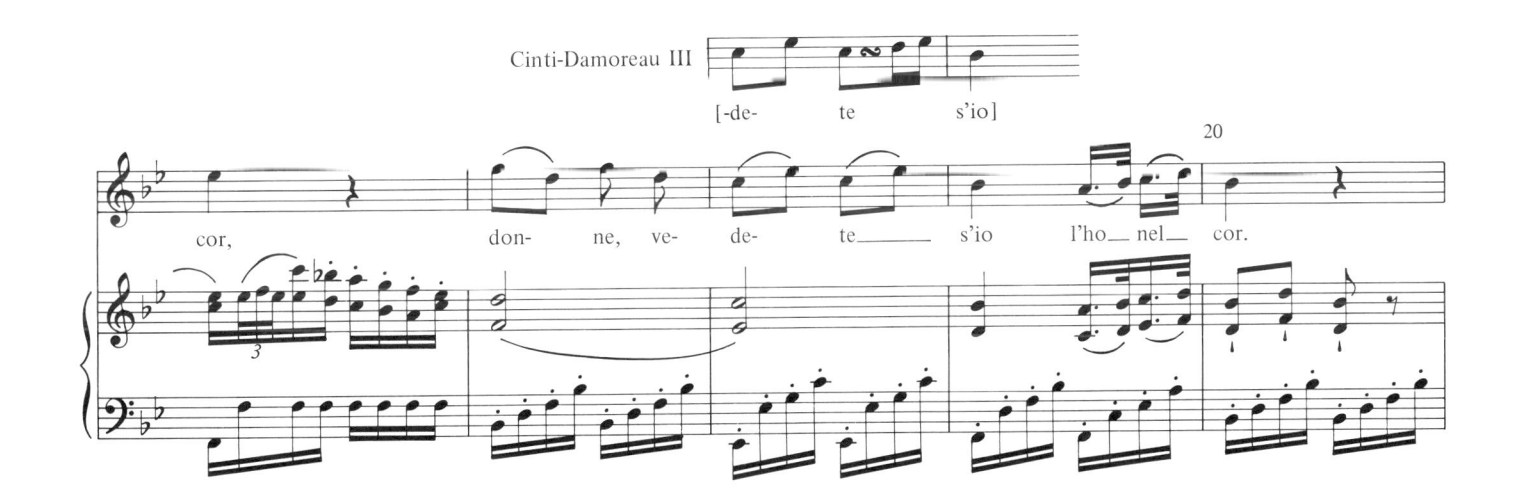

[vi ri- di- rò,]
Quel- lo ch'io pro- vo vi ri- di- rò, è per me
25
[ca- pir nol so]
nuo- vo, ca- pir nol so. Sen- to un af- fet- to
30
[ch'o- ra è di- let- to,]
pien di de- sir, ch'o- ra è di- let- to, ch'o- ra è mar-
35
-tir. Ge- lo e poi sen- to l'al- ma av- vam- par,
40

[-men- to tor-]

e in un mo- men- to tor- no a ge- lar. Ri- cer- co un

be- ne fuo- ri di me, non so chi'l tie- ne,

[non so cos' è.]

non so cos' è. So- spi- ro e ge- mo sen- za vo- ler, pal- pi- to e

tre- mo sen- za sa- per. Non tro- vo pa- ce not- te ne dì, ma pur mi pia- ce

[-sì.] *rall.*

lan- guir co- sì. Voi che sa- pe- te che co- sa è a- -mor, don- ne, ve- de- te s'io l'ho nel cor, don- ne, ve- de- te s'io l'ho nel cor, don- ne, ve- [-de- te s'io l'ho nel cor.] -de- te s'io l'ho nel cor.

[10] Dunque io son
(*Il barbiere di Siviglia*)

Gioachino Rossini

te, già lo sa- pe- vo pria di te, lo sa-
-pe- vo pria di te.)

FIGARO
Di Lin- do- ro il va- go og--get-to sie- te voi, bel- la Ro- si- na, sie- te vo- i, sie- te vo- i, bel- la Ro--si- na. (Oh che vol- pe so- pra- fi- na, oh che vol- pe so- pra--fi- na! ma l'a- vrà da far con me, sì, ma l'a-

-vrà da far con me, ma l'avrà da far con me.) Senti, senti... ma a Lindoro per parlar come si fa? Zitto, zitto, qui Lindoro per parlar vi or sarà. Zitto, zitto, qui Lindoro per parlar vi or sarà. Per parlarmi?... Bravo! bravo! Venga pur, ma con prudenza; io già moro, io già moro d'impa-

-zien-za! Ma che tar-da, co- sa fa? E-gli at- ten-de qual-che se- gno, po- ve--rin, del vo-stro af-fet-to; sol due ri- ghe di bi- gliet- to, sol due ri- ghe di bi--gliet-to, gli man-da-te e qui ver- rà, gli man- da- te e qui ver- rà, gli man--da- te, gli man-da-te e qui ver- rà. Che ne di- te? Non vor- rei... Su, co--rag-gio. Non sa- prei... Sol due ri- ghe... Mi ver-go-gno... Ma di che, ma di che? si sa! Presto, presto qua il biglietto. Un biglietto?... eccolo qua. Già era scritto!... ve' che bestia, ve' che bestia! Il maestro faccio a lei! Fortunati affetti miei, io comincio a respirar. Ah che in cattedra costei di malizia può dettar. Ah tu solo, amor, tu sei che mi devi conso-

-lar, che mi de- vi, che mi de- vi con- so- lar. Ah tu
FIGARO
Don- ne, don-ne e- ter- ni
90
so- lo a- mor, tu se- i che mi de- vi con- so-
De- i, chi v'ar- ri- va, chi v'ar- ri- va, chi v'ar- ri- va a in- do- vi-
Ah tu so- lo a- mor tu se- i che mi
Garcia, *Hints* (for mezzo soprano)
[Ah tu so- lo, a- mor, tu se- i che mi
f p f
[Ah tu so- lo, a- mor, tu se- i che mi
Ah tu so- lo a- mor mi
Garcia, *Hints* (for soprano)
tu mi de- vi
Ah tu sol mi de- vi
ROSINA
-lar. Ah tu so- lo, a- mor, tu se- i che mi
FIGARO
-nar? Don-ne, don-ne e-ter- ni De- i, chi v'ar- ri- va, chi v'ar-

de- vi con- so- lar.
de- vi con- so- lar.]
de- vi con- so- lar.]
de- vi con- so- lar.
ah con- so- lar.
con- so- lar.
95
de- vi con- so- lar. Sen- ti, sen- ti... ma a Lin- do- ro...
-ri- va, chi v'ar- ri- va a in- do- vi- nar? Qui ver-
pp
100
Ven- ga pur, ma con pru-
-rà! A mo men- ti per par- lar- vi qui sa rà.
cresc.
f

Marchisio: for- tu- na- ti af- fet- ti
for- tu- na- ti af- fet- ti

ROSINA / FIGARO / ROSINA
-den- za. Zit- to, zit- to, qui ver- rà. For- tu- na- ti af- fet- ti

mie- i io co- min- cio a re- spi- rar co-
mie- i io co- min- cio a re- spi- rar co-
mie- i, io co- min- cio a re- spi- rar, co-

99

Garcia, *Traité*

ah tu so- lo a- mor tu

ah tu so- lo a-

so- lo a- mor mi

Marchisio

-min- cio a re- spi- rar ah tu so- lo a- mor mi

-min- cio a re- spi- rar. ah tu so- lo a-

ROSINA

-min- cio a__ re- spi- rar. Ah tu so- lo, a- mor,__ tu__

FIGARO

Don- ne, don- ne, e- ter- ni De-

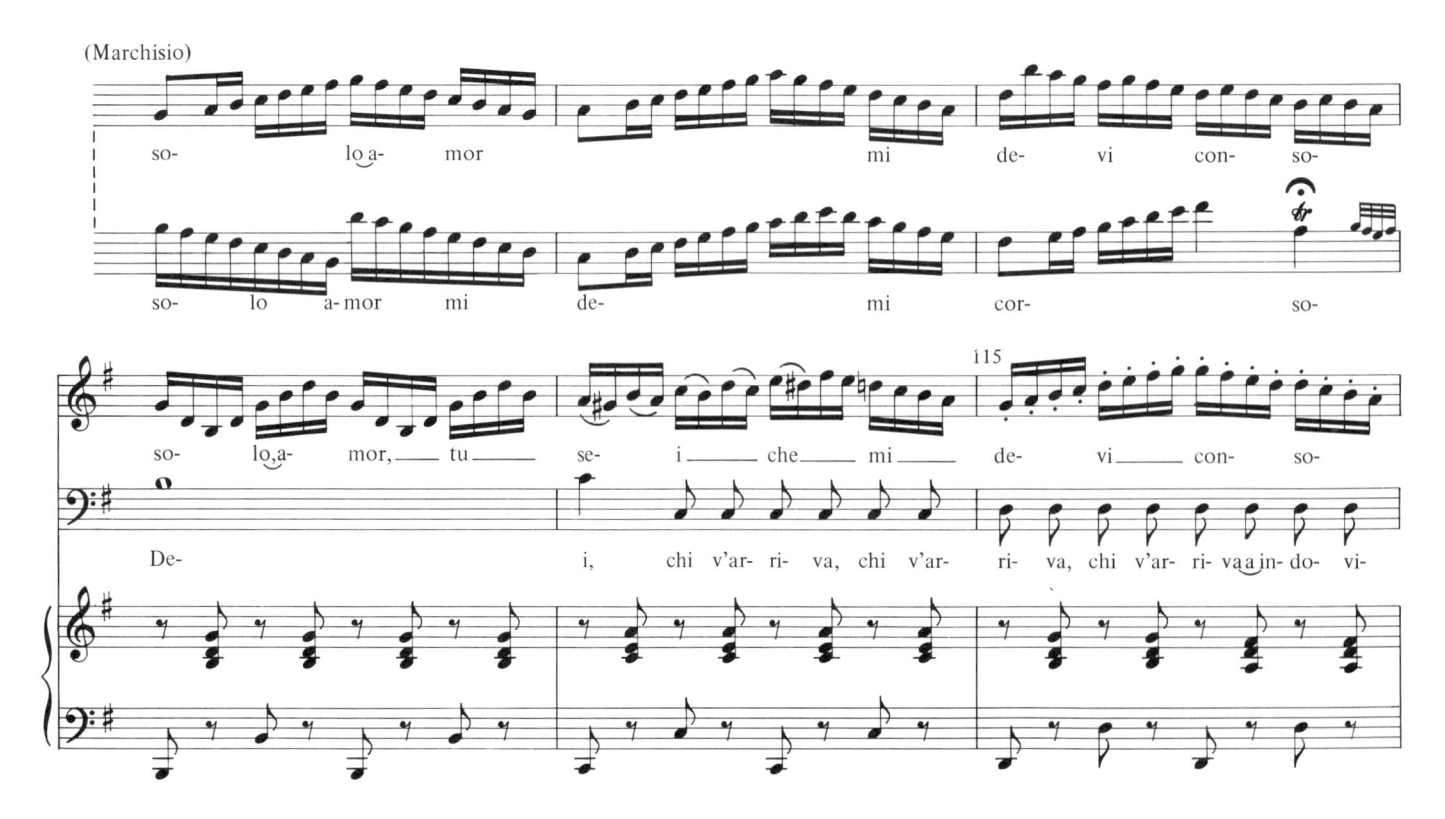

(Garcia) sei che mi devi consolar
-mor mi devi consolar
devi consolar

(Marchisio) devi consolar ah tu
-mor devi consolar ah tu

sei che mi devi consolar. Ah tu
-i, chi v'arriva, chi v'arriva, chi v'arriva a indovinar? Donne, donne, eterni

(Marchisio) solo amor mi devi conso-
solo amor mi devi cor so-

solo amor, tu sei che mi devi conso-
Dei, chi v'arriva, chi v'arriva, chi v'arriva a indovi-

-lar

-lar

-lar, che mi devi conso- lar, che mi
nar, chi v'ar- ri- va, chi v'ar-ri-va a in- do- vi- nar, chi v'ar-

de- vi conso- lar, sì, conso- lar, sì, conso-
-ri- va, chi v'ar-ri-va a in-do- vi- nar, a in- do- vi- nar, a in- do- vi-

-lar, sì, con- so- lar!
-nar, a in- do- vi- nar?

[11] Ecco ridente in cielo
(*Il barbiere di Siviglia*)

Gioachino Rossini

This edition includes the cavatina only (see Editorial Methods).

Garcia, *Traité*
Andante
sempre a tempo

ec- co ri-den- te il cie- lo spun- ta la bel- la au- ro-

15 ALMAVIVA

Ec- co ri-den- te in cie- lo spun- ta la bel- la au-

-ra e tu non sor- gi an- co- ra e

-ro- ra, e tu non sor- gi an- co- ra e _____

puoi dor- mir co- sì ah sor- gi mia bel- la

puoi dor- mir co- sì? _____ Sor- gi, mia dol- ce

*See Critical Notes.

cresc.
cresc.
dim.
spe- me vie- ni bel i- dol
25
spe- me, vie- ni, bell' i- dol
p
p
p
mi- o ren- di men cru- do di- o lo
mi- o, ren- di men cru- do, oh Di- o! lo
f
mf
sf
stral lo stral che mi fe- ri lo
a piacere
30
stral, lo stral che mi fe- ri, lo
f
stral che mi fe- ri
(Allegro)
stral che mi fe- ri.

[12a] Una voce poco fa
(Il barbiere di Siviglia)

Gioachino Rossini

ROSINA: U- na vo- ce po- co fa qui nel cor mi ri- suo- nò; il mio cor fe- ri- to è già, e Lin- do- ro fù che il pia-

-gò. Sì, Lindoro mio sarà, lo giurai, la vincerò. Sì, Lindoro mio sarà, lo giurai, la vincerò.

Il tutor ricuserà, io l'ingegno aguzzerò, alla fin s'accheterà, e contenta io resterò. Sì, Lindoro mio sarà, lo giurai, la vince-

Marchisio

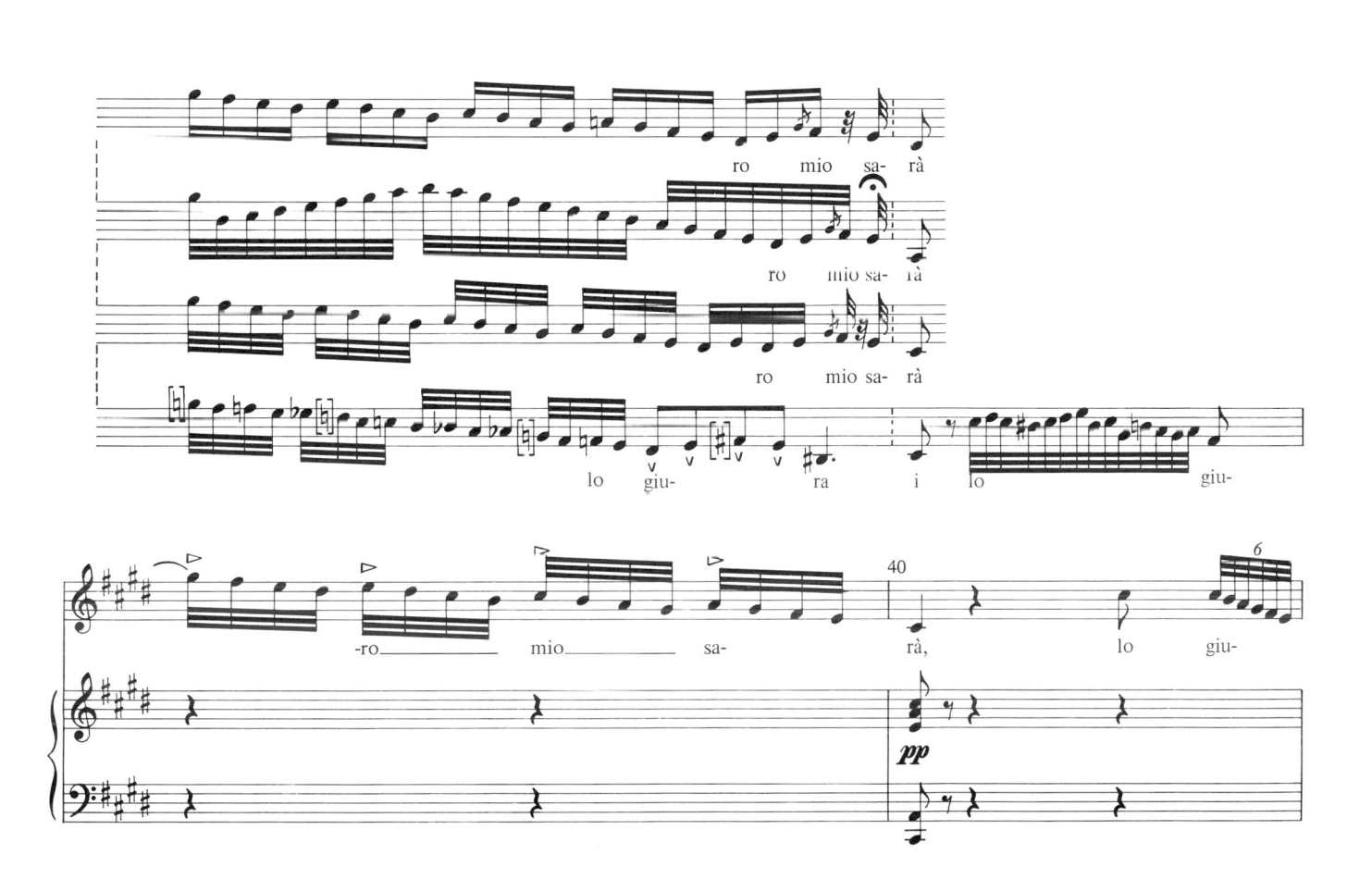

sì Lin- do-
sì Lin- do-
sì Lin- do-
sì Lin- do- ro sa- rà

rò. Sì, Lin- do-

ro mio sa- rà
ro mio sa- rà
ro mio sa- rà
lo giu- ra i lo giu-

-ro mio sa- rà, lo giu-

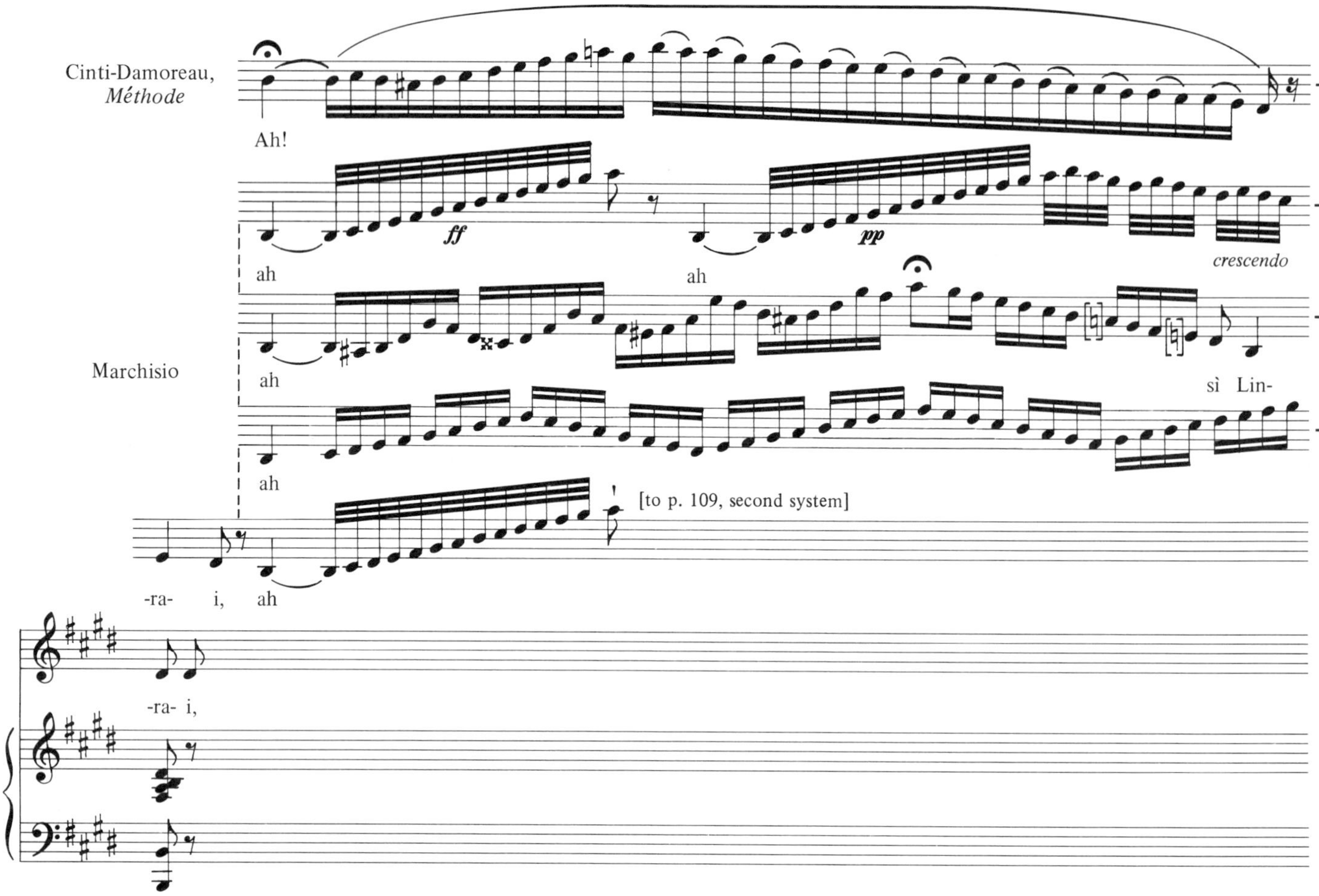
Cinti-Damoreau,
Méthode
Ah!
ah
ff
ah
pp
crescendo
Marchisio
ah
sì Lin-
ah
[to p. 109, second system]
-ra- i, ah
-ra- i,

109

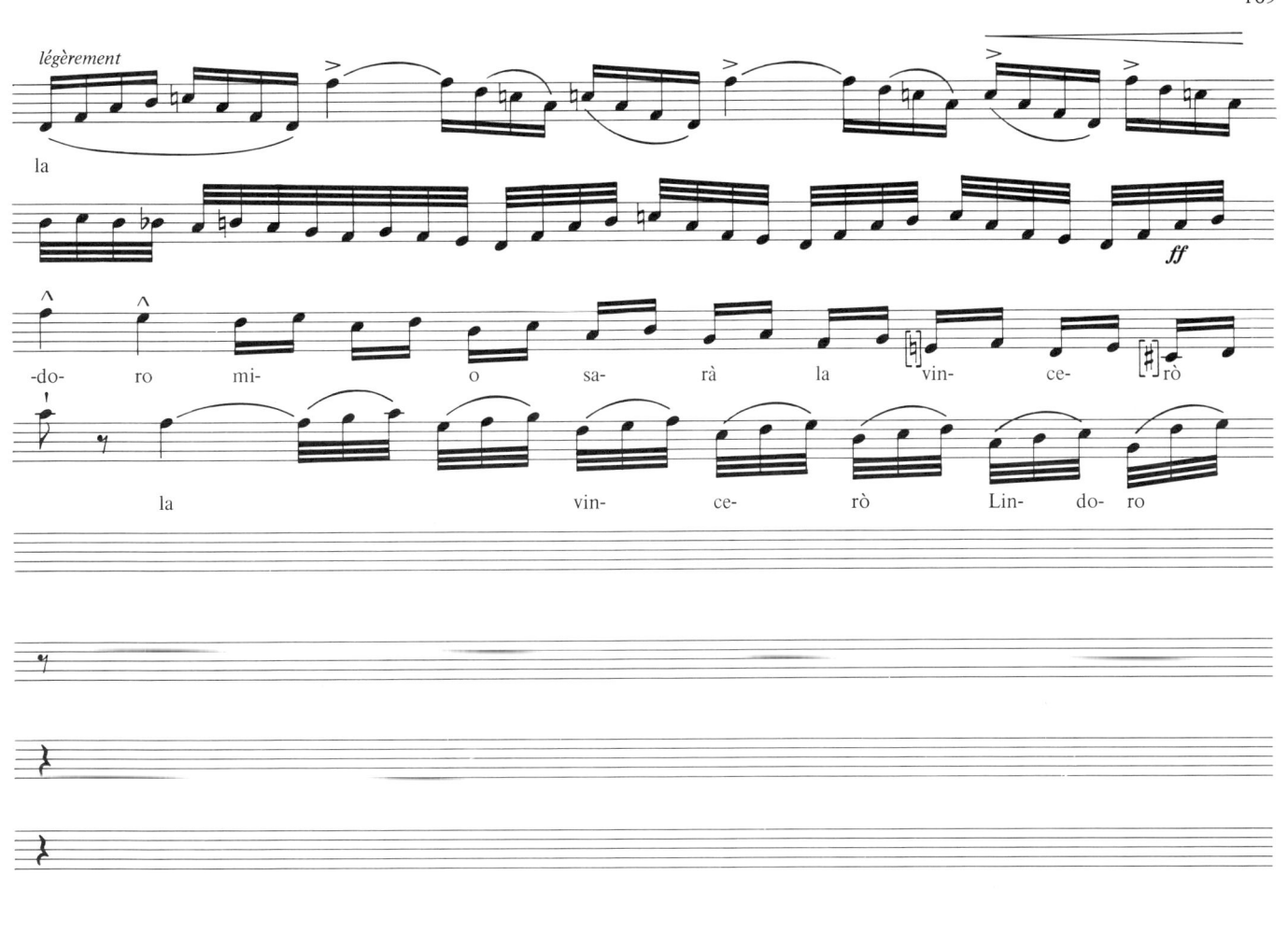

Io so-no do-ci-le, son ri-spet-to-sa, so-no ub-bi-dien-te, dol-ce, a-mo-ro-sa, mi la-scio

Marchisio: mi fò guidar mi fò guidar, regere, mi lascio regere, mi fò guidar, mi fò guidar ma ma se mi toccano dov'è il mio debole, sarò una vipera sarò, e cento trappole prima di vipera, sarò, e cento trappole prima di cedere farò giocar, cedere farò giocar, farò giocar, e cento trap- po- le pri- ma di ce- de- re fa- rò gio- car,___ fa- rò___ gio-

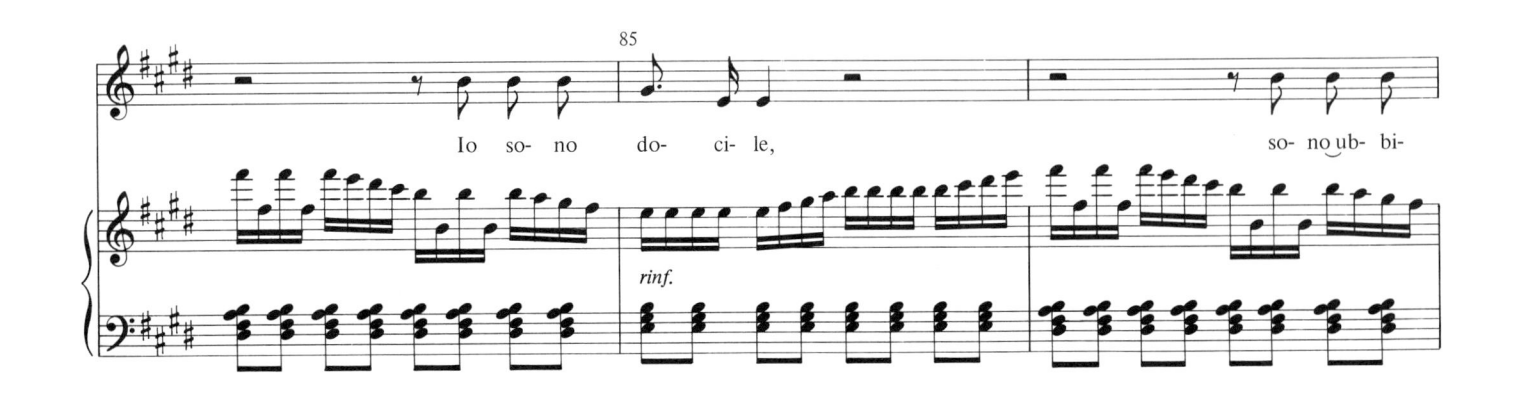

-car, e_ cen- to_ trap- po- le pri- ma di_ ce- de- re, e cen- to

trap- po- le fa- rò, fa- rò gio- car.

Io so- no do- ci- le, so- no ub- bimi fo gui- dar

-dien- te, mi la- scio reg- ge- re, mi fò gui- dar.

ma se mi toc- ca- no dov'è il mio de- bo- le, sa- rò u- na

Ma se mi toc- ca- no dov'è il mio de- bo- le, sa- rò u- na

vi- pe- ra sa- rò, e cen- to trap- po- le pri- ma di

vi- pe- ra, sa- rò, e cen- to trap- po- le pri- ma di

ce- de- re fa- rò gio- car

ce- de- re fa- rò gio- car,____ fa- rò____ gio- car, e cento

trap- po- le pri- ma di ce- de- re fa- rò gio- car, fa- rò____ gio- car, e___ cento___

trap- po-

trap- po-

trap- po- le pri- ma di___ ce- de- re, e cento trap- po- le fa-

-le fa- rò gio- rò, fa- rò gio- car, e cen-to trap- po-le fa- rò gio- car, e cen-to trap- po-le fa- rò gio- car, fa- rò gio- car, fa- rò gio- car, fa- rò gio- car.

[12b] Una voce poco fa

(*Il barbiere di Siviglia*)

Gioachino Rossini

vo- ce po- co fà qui nel cor mi ri- suo- nò il mio cor fe- ri- to è
vo- ce po- co fa qui nel cor mi ri- suo- nò; il mio cor fe- ri- to è
15
p
già e Lin- do- ro fù che il pia- gò. Si Lin- do- ro mio sa-
già, e Lin- do- ro fù che il pia- gò. Sì, Lin- do- ro mio sa-
20
f
mf
-rà, lo giu- ra- i, la vin- ce- rò, Si, Lin- do- ro mi- o sa-
-rà, lo giu- ra- i, la vin- ce- rò. Sì, Lin- do- ro mio sa-
25
pp

-rà, lo giu-ra-i, la vin-ce-rò.

Il tu-tor ri-cu-se-rà, Io l'in-ge-gno a-guz-ze-rò, Al-la fin s'ac-che-te-rà, e con-ten-ta io res-te-rò, Si Lin-do-ro mio sa-rà, lo giu-ra-i, la vin-ce-rò. si Lin-

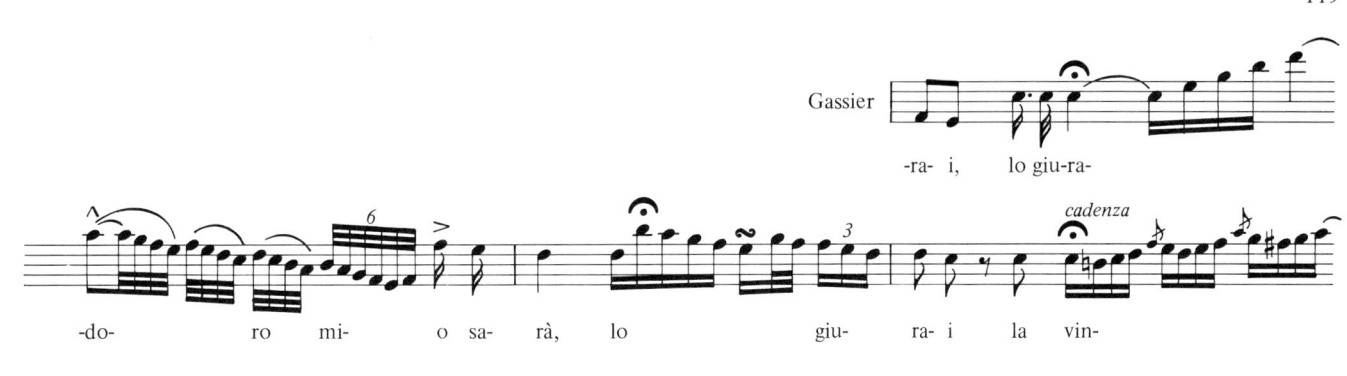

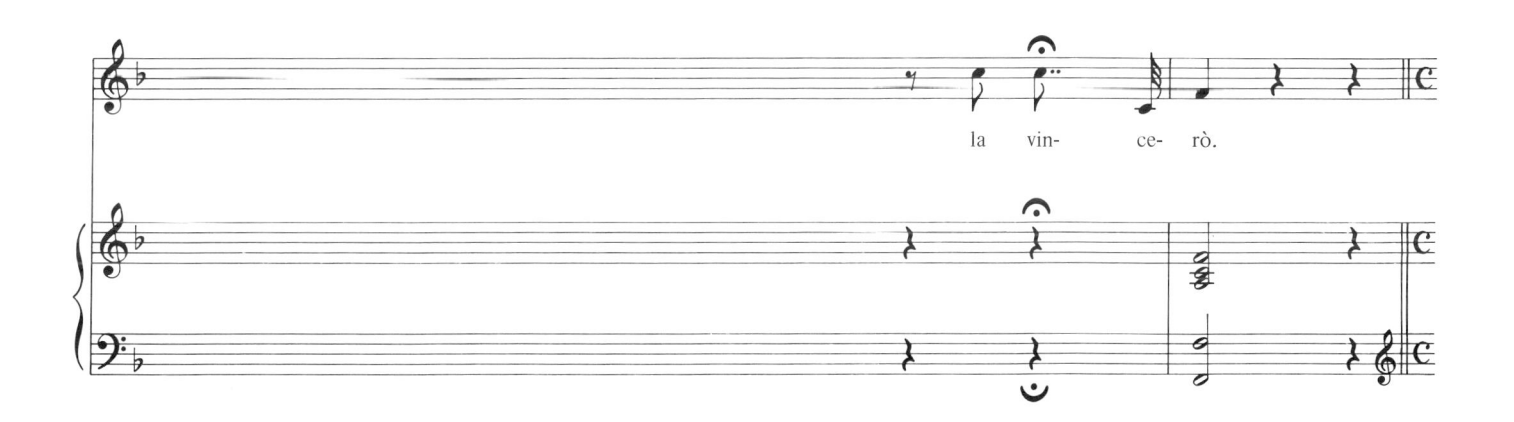

119

Gassier

-ra- i, lo giura-do- ro mi- o sa- rà, lo giura- i la vin-do- ro mio sa- rà, lo giura- i,

cadenza

i la vin- ce- rò
ce- rò.

la vin- ce- rò.

Lind: Io sono docile, son rispettosa,
Io sono docile, son rispettosa,
Sono obbediente, dolce, amorosa, Mi lascio
sono ubbidiente, dolce, amorosa, mi lascio

reg- ge- re, mi la- scio reg- ge- re, mi fò gui- dar, mi fò gui-
reg- ge- re, mi la- scio reg- ge- re, mi fò gui- dar, mi___ fò___ gui-

-dar. Ma se mi toc- ca- no dov'è il mio de- bo- le, co- me u- na
-dar. Ma se mi toc- ca- no dov'è il mio de- bo- le, sa- rò u- na

vi- pe- ra sa- rò, E cen- to trap- po- le pri- ma di
vi- pe- ra,___ sa- rò, e cen- to trap- po- le pri- ma di

ce- de- re, fa- rò gio- car, fa- rò gio- car, e cen- to
ce- de- re fa- rò gio- car,___ fa- rò___ gio- car, e cen- to

trap- po- le pri- ma di ce- de- re, farò gio- car farò gio-

-ca- re, e cento trap- po- le pri- ma di ce- de- re, e cento

trap- po- le fa- rò, fa- rò gio- car.

Io so- no do- ci- le, so- no ob- be-

-dien- te, mi lascio reggere mi fò guidar.

Gassier: Ma se mi toccano nel mio debole, sarò una
Ma se mi toccano dov' il mio debole come una
Ma se mi toccano dov' è il mio debole, sarò una
vipera sarò
vipera sarò, e cento trappole, prima di
vipera, sarò, e cento trappole prima di

(Lind)
ce- de- re, fa- rò gio- ca- re, e cen- to
ce- de- re fa- rò gio- car, fa- rò gio- car, e cen- to
con abandon
trap- po- le, pri- ma di ce- de- re fa- rò gio- car, fa- rò gio-
100
trap- po- le pri- ma di ce- de- re fa- rò gio- car, fa- rò gio-
-ca- re, e cen- to trap- po- le pri- ma di ce- de- re, e cen- to
-car, e cen- to trap- po- le pri- ma di ce- de- re, e cen- to
trap- po- le fa- rò gio- car, e cen- to
105
trap- po- le fa- rò, fa- rò gio- car, e cen- to
sf
sf

trap- po-le fa- rò gio- car, e cen- to trap- po-le fa- rò gio-
trap- po-le fa- rò gio- car, e___ cen- to trap- po-le fa- rò gio-

-car, fa- rò gio- -car, fa- rò gio- car, fa- rò gio-
-car, fa- rò gio -car, fa- rò gio- car,_ fa- rò gio-

-car.

-car.

[13] Nacqui all'affanno
(*La Cenerentola*)

Gioachino Rossini

Pasta: -frì ta- cen- do il

CENERENTOLA: Nac- qui al- l'af- fan- no e al pian- to sof- frì ta- cen- do il

co- re; ma per soave in-

sotto voce

[del- l'e- tà mia nel
-can- to dell' e- tà mia nel

fio- re,]
fio- re, co- me un ba- le- no

ff

ra- pi- do la sor- te mi- a, la sor- te mi- a can- giò,

p

[co- me un ba- le- no ra- pi- do]

co- me un ba- le- no ra- pi- do la sor- te

Cinti-Damoreau, *Méthode*

can- *lento* gio ah

mi- a, la sor- te mi- a can-

can-

Pasta
-gio
ter- ge-te il ci- glio [per-ché tre-
Allegro
-giò. No, no, no, no! ter-ge-te il ci- glio, per-ché tre-
stacc.
mar, per ché tre- mar, per- ché?]
[a que-sto
-mar, per- ché tre- mar, per- ché? A que-sto sen, a que-sto
sen] vo- la- te,
sen vo- la- te, fi- glia, so- rel- la, a-
-mi- ca, tut- to, tut- to, tut- to, tut- to tro- va- te in

130

me, tro- va- te, tro- va- te in me.

Pasta
[Non più

Non più mesta ac- can- to al fuo- co sta- rò so- la a gor- gheg- giar, no! Ah, fu un

mesta ac- can- to al fuo- co sta- rò so- la a gor- gheg- giar, no! Ah, fu un

lam- po un so- gno un gio- co il mi- o] lun- go pal- pi- tar
60
lam- po un so- gno un gio- co il mi- o lun-go pal-pi- tar.
p
non più
65
Non più me- sta ac-can- to al fuo- co, non più
me- sta ac- can- to al fuo- co [sta- rò so- la a gor- gheg-
70
me- sta ac-can- to al fuo- co sta- rò so- la a gor- gheg-
-giar, no! Ah, fu un lam- po, un so- gno, un gio- co] Il mio
-giar, no! Ah, fu un lam- po un so- gno un gio- co il mio
f
p

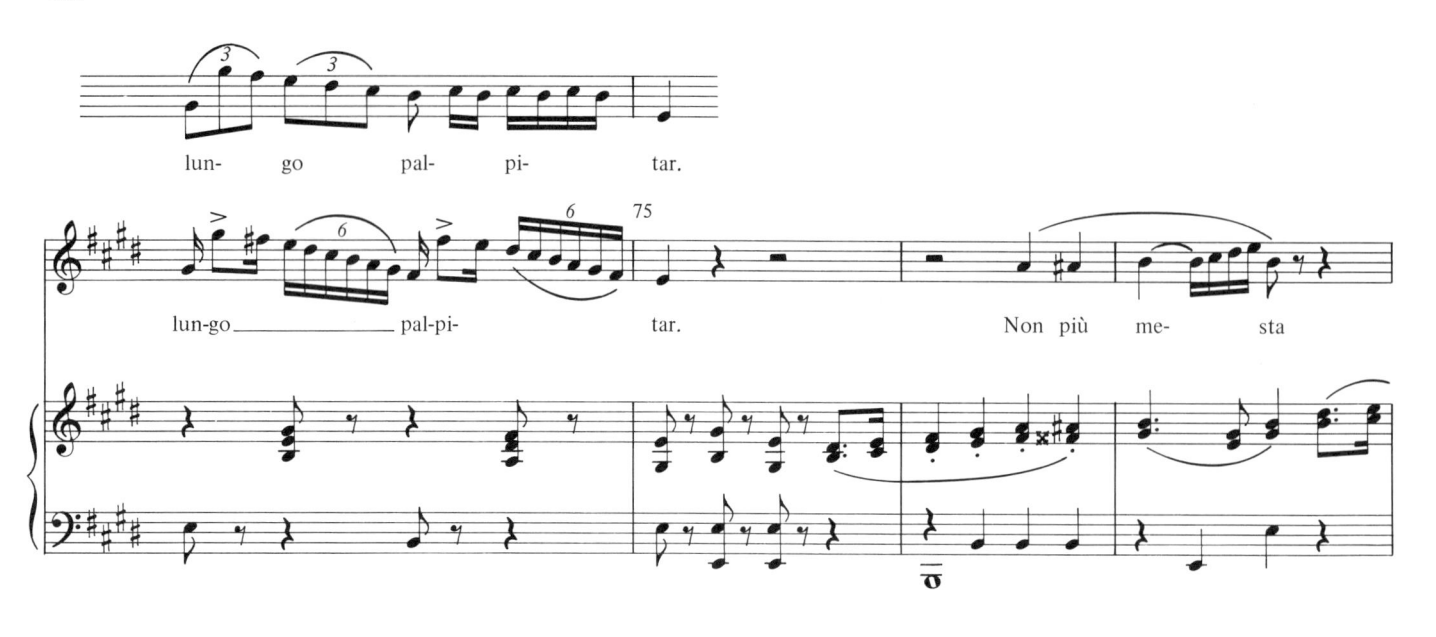

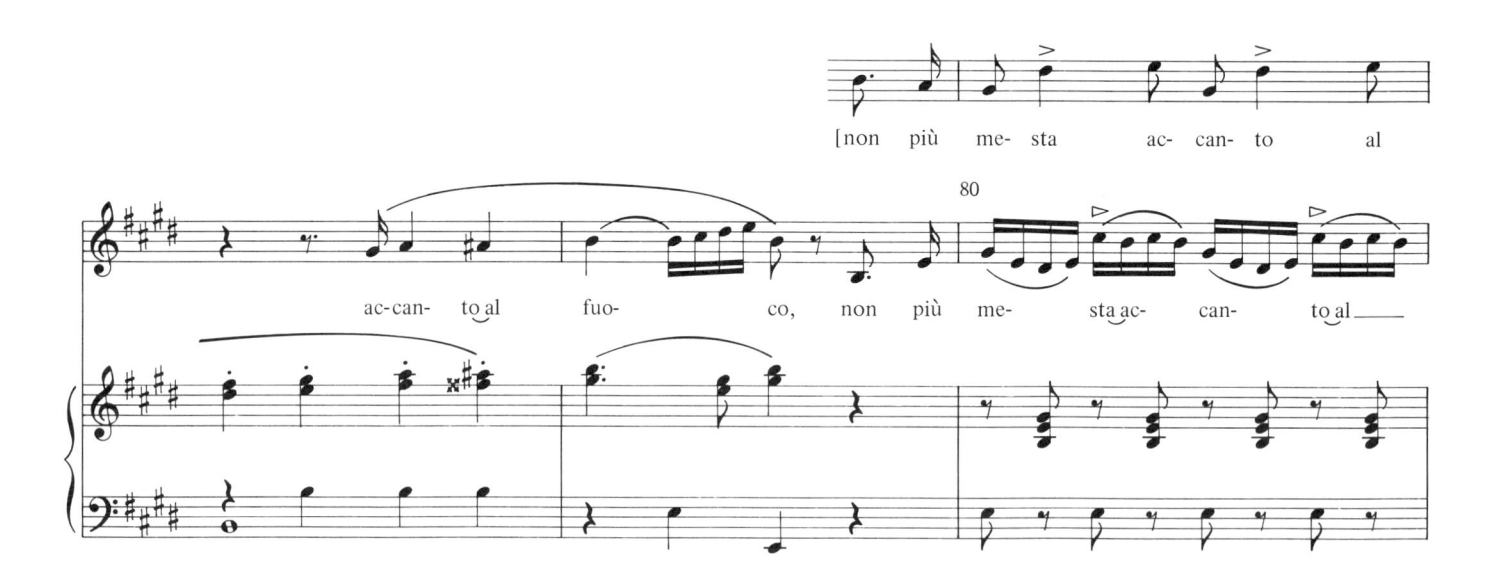

lun- go pal- pi- tar.

lun-go _____ pal-pi- tar. Non più me- sta

[non più me- sta ac- can- to al

ac-can- to al fuo- co, non più me- sta ac- can- to al _____

fuo- co] sta-rò so- la a gor-gheg- giar [Ah, fu un

fuo- co _____ sta-rò _____ so- la a _____ gor-gheg- giar. Ah, fu un

[ossia] lun- go pal- pi-

lam- po, un so- gno, un gio- co Il mio lun- go pal- pi-
lam- po, un so- gno, un gio- co il mio lun- go pal- pi-

-tar.
-tar. Ah, fu un lam- po,] un so gno un gio-
-tar. Ah, fu un lam- po, un so-gno un gio-

-co ah fu un lam- po un so- gno un gio- co il mio lun- go il mio
-co, ah, fu un lam- po, un so- gno, un gio- co il mi- o lun- go

lun- go pal- pi- tar
95
pal- pi- tar. Ah, fu un lam- po, un so- gno un
ah, fu un lam- po un so- gno un gio- co il mio
100
gio- co, ah, fu un lam- po un so- gno un gio- co il mi- o
[3]
lun- go il mio lun- go pal- pi- tar.
105
lun- go pal- pi- tar. Ah, fu un
gio- co, ah, fu un gio- co, ah, fu un lam-
f

-po, il pal- pi- tar, ah, fu un gio- co, ah, fu un gio- co, ah, fu un lam- -po, il pal- pi- tar, il mio lungo palpitar, il mio lungo palpi- tar, il pal- pi- tar, il pal- pi- tar, il pal- pi-

-tar.

[14] Di piacer mi balza il cor
(*La gazza ladra*)

Gioachino Rossini

Di piacer mi balza il cor; ah! bramar di più non so: e l'amante e il genitor finalmente io rive-

Cinti-Damoreau III*

Sur son coeur l'un me pres-se-ra, dans mes bras l'autre vo-le-ra

ce- lui que j'a-

-drò, io ri- ve- drò, io ri- ve--drò.

L'u- no al sen mi strin-ge--ra; l'al- tro, l'al- tro, ah! che fa- rà? Dio d'a- mor, con-fi- do in te; deh, tu pre- mia la mia fè! Dio d'a- mor, con-fi- do in

*Concerning the French text of Cinti-Damoreau's embellishments, see Texts and Translations.

Andante
[autre]
m'ait
gar- dé [gar-
autre
rall.
m'ait
gar- dé, gar-
-do-re
m'ait
gar- dé
te; deh,
tu
pre-mia
-dé]
-dé
sa
Ah
sa
40
la
mia
col canto

foi
foi
du plai- sir l'ai- ma- ble i-
fè! Di pia- cer mi bal- za il cor; ah! bra- mar di più non
a tempo
-vres- se
et mon pè- re et mon a-
45
so: e l'a- man- te e il ge- ni- tor fi- nal- men- te io ri- ve-
-mant.
50
-drò, io ri- ve- drò,

io ri- ve- drò.

Tut- to sor-

l'at-ten- te

-ri- de- re mi veg-go in-tor- no; più lie- to

giorno, brillar non può, no, no, no, no, non può,

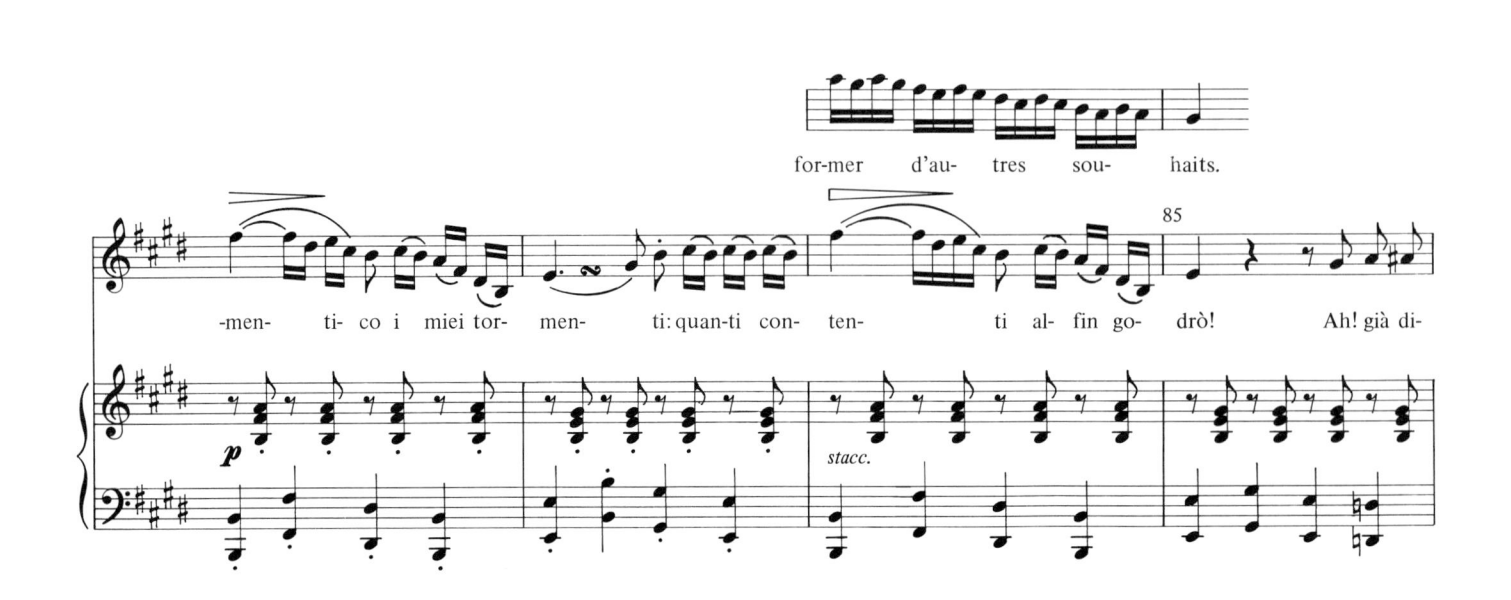

più lieto giorno, più lieto

giorno brillar non può, no, no, no, no, non può. Ah! già di-

-mentico i miei tormenti: quanti contenti al fin godrò! Ah! già di-

former d'autres souhaits.

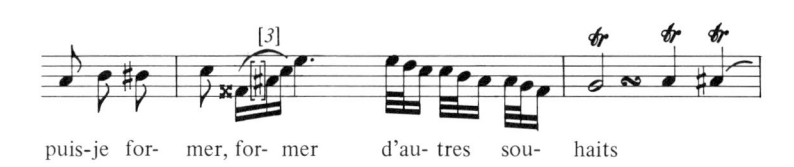

puis-je for- mer, for- mer d'au- tres sou- haits

-men-ti- co i miei tor- men- ti: quan-ti con- ten- ti, sì, al- fin go- drò!

oui tout m'en-chan- te l'at-ten- te

Tut- to sor- ri- de- re mi veg- go in- tor- no;

più lie- to gior- no bril-lar non può, no, no, no, no, non può,

[autre]
ja- mais l'at- ten- te
ja- mais l'at- [ten-] te
100
più lie- to gior- no,
stacc.
pour une a- man- te
più lie- to gior- no bril-lar non può, no, no,
pp
[autre]
puis-je for-
puis-je for-
105
no, no, non può. Ah! già di- men- ti- co i miei tor- men- ti: quan-ti con-
p

-mer d'au- tres sou- haits

-mer d'au- tres sou- haits non plus de pei- nes plus de tris-

-ten- ti al- fin go- drò! Ah! già di- men- ti- co i miei tor-

-tes- se puis- je for- mer

-men- ti: quan- ti con- ten- ti al- fin go- drò! Ah! già di-

-men- ti co i miei tor- men- ti: quan- ti con- ten- ti al- fin go-

-drò, al- fin go- drò, al- fin go- drò,

al- fin go- drò, al- fin go-

ten-dres-

-drò, al- fin go- drò, al-

-se

-fin go- drò, al- fin god'au- tres sou- haits

-drò, al- fin ___ go- drò, al- fin go-

[-haits, d'au- tres] sou- haits d'au- tres sou- haits

-drò, al- fin go- drò, al- fin go- drò!

[15] Sombre forêt
(*Guillaume Tell*)

Gioachino Rossini

-ment ap- pren- dra mes se- crets, ap- -pren- -dra mes se- crets, mes se- crets.

Toi, du ber- -ger as- tre doux et ti mi de, Qui sur mes pas viens se- mant tes re- flets, Ah, sois aus-

-si mon é- toile et mon gui- de. Com- me lui, tes ray- ons, tes ray- ons sont dis- crets; Et l'é- cho seu- le- ment re- di- ra mes se- crets, re- di- ra mes se- crets, mes se- crets, l'é- cho seul re- di- ra, re- di- ra mes se- crets, l'é- cho seul re- di-

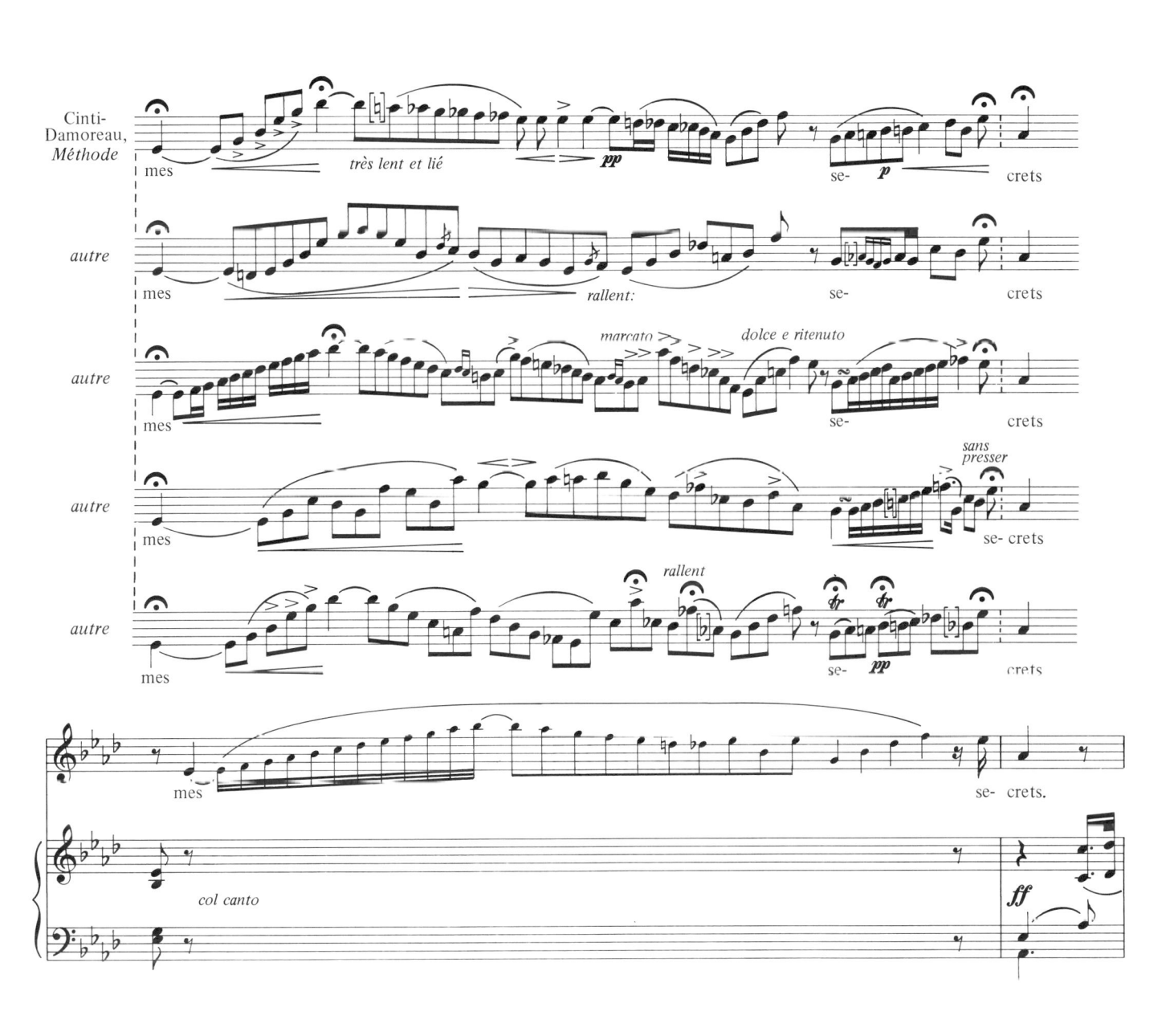

Cinti-Damoreau, Méthode: mes — très lent et lié — se- crets

autre: mes — rallent: — se- crets

autre: mes — marcato — dolce e ritenuto — se- crets

autre: mes — sans presser — se- crets

autre: mes — rallent — se- crets

mes se- crets.

col canto

[16] Pensa alla patria
(*L'italiana in Algeri*)

Gioachino Rossini

ve- di per tut- ta I- ta- lia ri- na- sce- re gli e-
ca-res- se pro- fon- de i-vres-
[-ta- lia] [-sce- re de i-vres-gli e-

-sem- pi d'ar- dir e di va- lor, sì, d'ar-
-se c'est lui je
-sem-] [sì, d'ar-

vais je vais le voir
-di- re e di va- lor,

ve- di per tut- ta I- ta- lia gli e- sem- pi d'ar-
quel- le i-
[d'ar-

-vres- se ah quel- le i- vres- se je
-dir, ah, d'ar- dir, ah,
-dir e di

vais e di va- le [voir.]
lor.]
va- lor.

Allegro

Sciocco! tu ri- di? sciocco! tu ri- di an-

-co- ra? Van- ne, mi fai di- spet- to, van- ne, mi fai di- spet- to, mi fai di-
-spet- to. Ca- ro, ca- ro, ca- ro, ti par li in pet- to a-
je [a-
trou- ve je trou- ve
-mo- re, do- ve- re, trou- ve- re,]
-mo- re, do- ve- re, a- mor, do- ve- re, o- nor. A-
-mi- ci in o- gni e ven- to... Vi- ci- no è già il mo-

-men- to... Se poi va ma- le il gio- co...

Qual pia- cer! Fra po-chi i- stan- ti, fra po-chi i- stan- ti ri-ve-

je bé- nis
[(Nel pe- ri-]
-drem le pa- trie a- re- ne. (Nel pe- ri- glio del___ mio

porte a- vec or- gueil.
[-gio- sa a- a- mor mi fa.]

be- ne, del mio be- ne co- rag- gio- sa a- mor mi fa. Nel pe-

-ri- glio del mio be- ne co- rag- gio- sa a- mor mi

fa, co- rag- gio- sa, co- rag- gio- sa, co- rag-

-gio- sa a- mor mi fa, co- rag- gio- sa, co- rag-

a- vec or- gueil
[-gio- sa a- mor mi fa.)]
90
-gio- sa, co- rag- gio- sa a- mor mi fa.)
95
cresc.
100
105
110
Qual pia-

dol.
[ri- ve- drem le pa- trie a-
-cer! Fra po-chi i stan- ti, fra po-chi i- stan- ti ri- ve- drem le pa- trie a-
dol.
sostenuto
je te bé- nis les dou-ces chaî- nes les dou-ces
-re- ne. (Nel pe- ri-] [del mio be- ne, del mio
113
-re- ne. (Nel pe- ri- glio del mio be- ne, del mio
chaî- nes que je porte a- vec or- gueil.
be- ne co- rag- gio- sa a- mor mi fa.]
120
be- ne co- rag- gio- sa a- mor mi fa. Nel pe- ri- glio del mio
pp
âme a fui le deuil fiè- re de mes
[-gio- sa a- mor mi fa,] [-gio- sa, co- rag-
125
be- ne co- rag- gio- sa a- mor mi fa, co- rag- gio- sa, co- rag-
f p

[!]
chaî- nes je les por- te a- vec or- gueil je suis
-gio- sa, co- ra- gio- sa a- mor mi fa,] [co- rag-
-gio- sa, co- rag- gio- sa a- mor mi fa, co- rag-
fiè- re de mes chaî- nes je les por- te a- vec or-
-gio- sa, co- rag- gio- sa, co- rag- gio- sa a- mor mi
130
-gio- sa, co- rag- gio- sa, co- rag- gio- sa a- mor mi
-gueil
fa.]
135
fa. Nel pe- ri- glio del mio be- ne co- rag-
je suis fiè- re de mes
[Nel pe- ri- glio del mio
-gio- sa a- mor mi fa. Nel pe- ri- glio del mio

chaî- nes je les por- te,
be- ne co- rag- gio- sa]
140
be- ne co- rag- gio- sa a-mor mi fa, a- mor mi
f p
f p
ff
fa, a- mor mi fa, a- mor mi fa, a- mor mi
145
sf
sf sf sf sf
sf sf sf sf
-gueil a- vec or- gueil
fa, a- mor mi fa.)]
fa, a- mor mi fa.)
sf sf sf
150

[17] Parlar, spiegar
(*Mosè in Egitto*)

Gioachino Rossini

OSIRIDE: Par- lar, spie- gar non pos- -so quel che nel pet- to io sen- to, quel che nel pet- to io sen- to. Ah! no...del mi- o, del mio tor- men- to dar-si non può, non può mag- gior. Ah! no...del mio tor-

-men- to dar-si,___ dar-si non può mag- gior,___ dar-si non può___ mag- gior, dar-si non può mag- gior, dar-si non può mag- gior!

FARAONE: È il ciel per noi se- re- no, se pria fu_av- ver- so_e fie- ro, se pria fu_av- ver- so_e fie- ro:

Ti calmerà, sì, sì, lo spero, dolce e soave amor Ti calmerà, lo spero, dolce, dolce, soave amor, dolce, soave amor, dolce, soave amor. No... sempre sventurato... Per-

-chè? Qual tri-sto e-ven- to? Pa- dre! Ah! non sa- i... Fa-

-vel- la... La mia ne-mi- ca stel- la mi

vuo- le op-pres- so o- gnor. È a te ra-gion ru-

-bel- la? Nè ti com-pren- do an- cor, nè

ti com-pren- do an- cor, an-

-cor. Fa- vel- la, fa- vel- la!

(Non mer- ta più con- si- glio il

mi- se- ro mio sta- to;

Tamburini
Pal- pi- to a quell' as- pet- to a quel as-

FA.
(Pal- pi- to a quell' a- spet- to, a quell' a-

è il più cru- del pe-

-pet- to
-spet- to! Ge- mo nel suo do- lor!

Rubini
-ri- glio vo in-
(OS.)
-ri- glio vo in- tre- pi- do a sfi- dar.
(FA.)
Ah! qual sa- rà l'og-
Tamburini
-rà del gra- ve su- o pe-
-get- to, qual sa- rà, del gra- ve suo pe-
110
OS.
115
È il piu crù- del, cru- del pe- ri- glio,
-nar
FA.
-nar?
Ah! qual sa- rà, sa- rà l'og- get- to
pp
f
cresc.

sì, sì, vo in- tre- pi- do a sfi- dar, è il più cru-del pe-
del gra- ve suo pe- nar?
-ri- glio vo in-tre- pi- da, vo in- tre- pi- do, vo in-tre- pi- do a sfi-
Ah! qual sa- rà l'og- get- to, ah! qual sa- rà l'og- get- to del gra- ve suo pe-
-dar, in- tre- pi- do a sfi- dar.) Non
-nar, del suo pe- nar?) Ma che t'af-fan- na?
pos- so, Pa- dre . . . Ah! non sa- i . . . La mia ne-mi- ca
Fa-vel- la . . .

stel- la ... mi vuo- le op-pres- so o- gnor. È a

te ragion ru- bel- la? Nè ti com-pren- do an-

-cor. Fa- vel- la, fa- vel- la...

Rubini
-si- glio il

os. (Non mer- ta più con- si- glio il

mi- se- ro mio sta- to
(OS.)
mi- se- ro mio sta- to;
150
FA.
(Pal- pi- to a quell' a- spet- to a quell' a-
è il più cru- del pe-
Tamburini
spet- to ge- mo nel suo do- lor
-spet- to! Ge- mo nel suo do- lor!
pp
Rubini
155 -ri- glio vo in- tre- pi- do a sfi- dar
-ri- glio vo in- tre- pi- do a sfi- dar.
Tamburini
-get- to qual sa-
Ah! qual sa-rà l'og- get- to, qual sa-

Ou
gra- ve suo pe- nar
-rà del gra- ve suo pe- nar
160
-rà, del gra- ve suo pe- nar?
pp
OS.
FA.
165
È il più cru- del, cru- del pe- ri- glio,
Ah! qual sa- rà, sa- rà l'og- get- to
f
cresc.
170
sì, sì, vo in- tre- pi- do a- sfi- dar, è il più cru- del pe- ri-
del gra- ve suo pe- nar? Ah! qual sa- rà l'og-
f
ff
-glio vo in- tre- pi- do, vo in- tre- pi- do, vo in- tre- pi- do a sfi- dar, in- tre- pi-
-get- to, ah! qual sa- rà l'og- get- to del gra- ve suo pe- nar, del
ppp

175
-do a sfi- dar, vo in- tre- pi-do a sfi- dar, vo in-
suo pe- nar, del gra- ve suo pe- nar, del
ff
180
-tre- pi-do a sfi- dar, vo in- tre- pi- do a sfi- dar, vo in-
gra- ve suo pe- nar, del gra- ve suo pe- nar, del
-tre- pi- do a sfi- dar.)
gra- ve suo pe- nar?)
185

[18] "Assisa a pie"
(Otello)

Gioachino Rossini

DESDEMONA
con espressione
"As- si- sa a piè d'un sa- li- ce, im- mer- sa nel do- lo- re, ge-
-mea tra-fit- ta l- sau- ra dal più cru-de- le a- mo- re: L'au- ra fra i ra- mi
fle- bi- le ne ri- pe- te- va il suon.
"I ru-scel-let- ti lim- pi- di a'

175

[di mie sciagure immemore]
immemore all'-presta, di mie sciagure immemore, all'urna mia funesta urna mia funesta; nè più ripeta l'aura de' miei lamenti il suon de' miei lamenti il suon." Che dissi!... Ah! m'ingannai!... Non è del canto questo il lugubre fin. M'ascolta...

Oh Dio! Qual mai strepito è questo! Qual presagio funesto! Non paventar; rimira: Impetuoso vento è quel, che s'unisce a miei lamenti spira. Io credeva che alcuno... Oh come il Cielo s'unisce a' miei lamenti!...

178

Moderato

fa. Par- ti, ri- ce- vi da' lab-bri dell' a-
-mi- ca il ba- cio e-stre- mo.

EMILIA
Ah che di- ci! Ub- bi- di- sco... oh co- me tre- mo!

Larghetto

DESDEMONA
Deh cal- ma, o Ciel, nel son- no per po- co le mie pe- ne, fa', che l'a- ma- to be- ne mi ven- ga a con- so-

-lar. Se poi son vani i prieghi, di mia breve urna in seno di pianto venga almeno il cenere a bagnar, sì, sì, il cenere a bagnar.

[19] Ah, quel giorno ognor rammento
(*Semiramide*)

Gioachino Rossini

-heur
-bar.]
20
-bar. L'in- vo- la- va, l'in- vo-
ff
p stacc.
-la- va in que- ste bracc- cia al suo vi- le, al suo
-lè- bre l'heu- reux vain- queur
[vi- le ra- pi- to-]
25
vi- le ra- pi- to- re; io sen- ti- a con- tro il mio
dol.
les sou- pirs de mon coeur
[pal- pi- tar, pal- pi- tar,]
co- re il suo co- re pal- pi- tar, io sen-

183

come da quel dì tut- to, tut- to per me can- giò, can- giò; quel guar- do mi ra- pì, sì, quest' a- ni- ma av- vam- pò. Il cie- lo per me s'a- prì, a- mo- re si m'a- ni- mò. D'A- ze- ma, di quel dì, no, no, no, no, scor- dar- mi io mai sa- prò, no mai, no mai, no mai sa- prò, scor- dar- mi mai, no mai sa-

70
-prò,
non sa-
prò,
p
ff
p
le sou- ve- nir
[non sa- prò.]
non sa- prò.
75
Schiu- se il ci- glio . . .
ff
p
stacc.
mi guar- dò . . .
80
mi sor- ri- se . . .
cresc.
pal- pi- tò.
Schiu- se il ci- glio . . .
f
85
mi guar- dò . . .
pal- pi- tò,
mi guar-
ff

90
-dò . . . pal- pi- tò, mi guar- dò . . .
[-do . . .]
dim.
mi guar- dò . . . Oh! co- me da quel
p
stacc.
[3] [3]
bien- tôt va te re- voir dè- ja son â- me s'a-ban-
[-tu, tut- to per me can- giò, can- giò; quel guar-do mi ra-
95
dì tut- to, tut- to per me can- giò, can- giò; quel guar- do mi ra-
-don- ne au plus flat- teur es- poir.
-pì, sì quest' a- ni- ma av-vam- pò.]
100
-pì, sì, quest' a- ni- ma av- vam- pò. Il cie- lo per- me s'a-
ff

-prì, a- mo- re si m'a-ni- mò. D'A- ze- ma, di quel dì, no, no, no, no, scor- dar- mi io mai sa- prò, no mai, no mai, no mai sa- prò,

[scor- dar- mi mai, no mai le sou- ve- nir -prò,]

scor- dar- mi mai, no mai sa- prò, non sa- prò,

le sou- ve- nir.
[-prò, no mai]
115
non sa- prò, no mai sa-
-drai le
[-prò, no mai]
-prò, no mai sa- prò, no mai sa-
120
-drai le sou- ve- nir
[-prò, no mai, no mai sa- prò.]
-prò, no mai sa- prò, no mai sa- prò.
125

[20] Du séjour de la lumière

(*Le siège de Corinthe*)

Gioachino Rossini

PAMIRA

Du sé- jour____ de la lu- miè- re Dai- gne, hé- las,____ ma ten- dre_ mè- re Ac- cueil- lir____ ma pri- è- re Et_ veil- ler___ sur__ mon des-

-tin. Du séjour de la lumière Daigne hélas, ma tendre

Cinti-Damoreau II

mère mère Accueillir ma prière Et veiller sur mon des-

-tin. Du séjour de la lumière Daigne hé-

-las ma tendre mère
-las, ma tendre mère, daigne, hé-

-las ma tendre mère

ac- cueillir ma prière

veiller sur mon destin Et veiller sur mon destin, veiller sur mon destin, et veil-

-ler sur mon des- tin, et veil-ler sur mon des- tin, et veil-

veil-ler sur mon des-

-tin

-tin.

Più mosso

Mais a- près un long o- ra- ge, un long o- ra- ge,

de l'es-cla- va- ge
A l'a- bri de l'es-cla- va- ge,
Ma pa- tri- e, ô doux, ô doux pré- sa- ge, Re-ver-
-ra ses plus beaux jours, re- ver- ra ses plus beaux jours, re- ver-
-ra ses
f p
f

plus beaux jours, ses plus beaux jours.

Meno mosso

Mais après un long o-ra-ge, un long o-ra-ge, un long o-ra-ge, A l'a-

[-bri] de l'es-cla-va-ge, -bri de l'es-cla-va-ge, Ma pa-

-tri- e, ô doux, ô doux pré- sa- ge, Re- ver-
90
ver-ra ses plus beaux
-ra ses plus beaux jours, re- ver- ra ses plus beaux
jours
95
jours, re- ver- ra
ses plus beaux jours, ses
100
plus beaux jours, Ma pa- trie, ô doux pré-
cresc.

-sa- ge, Re- ver- ra ses plus beaux jours, re- ver-ra, re- ver-ra ses plus beaux jours, ses plus beaux jours, re- ver- ra ses plus beaux jours, ses plus beaux jours, oui, re- ver- ra ses plus beaux jours.

[21] Di tanti palpiti
(*Tancredi*)

Gioachino Rossini

Anonymous: O patria dolce e ingrata patria al fin a té ri-

Gregoire: Oh patria dolce Ingrata Patria al fi- ne a te ri-

Recitativo
TANCREDI: Oh patria! dolce e ingrata patria! al fi- ne a te ri-

(Anon.)
-tor- no io ti sa- lu- to o ca- ra ter- ra De- gli a- vi mie- i ti
(Greg.)
lento
-tor- no Io ti sa- lu- to o ca- ra ter- ra de- gli a- vi mie- i ti
25
-tor- no! Io ti. sa- lu- to, o ca- ra ter- ra de- gli a- vi mie- i: ti
dolce
Cinti-Damoreau II
un nou- vel
[gior- no se-
ba- cio e que- sto per mé gior- no se-
animato
ba- cio e que- sto per me gior- no se-
ba- cio. È que- sto per me gior- no se-
ê- tre
-re- no]
Ah je me
[a re- spi-
-re- no Co- min- cia il cor á res- pi-
-re- no co- min- cia il co- re a re- spi-
30
-re- no: co- min- cia il cor a re- spi-

sens- ra-rmi in se- re nai- no.] tre

-rar- mi in se- no

-rar- mi in se- no.

Allegro

Gregoire: A- me- na- i- de

A- me- na- i- de!

o mio pen-sier so- a- ve so- lo de miei sos- pi- ri

O mio pen-sier so- a- ve, so- lo de' miei so- spir,

devoti miei celeste oggetto
de' voti miei celeste oggetto,

Io venni alfine io voglio Sfidando il mio destino qualunque ei sia meritarti o perire anima mia
io venni alfin: io voglio, sfidando il mio destino, qualunque sia, meritarti, o perir, anima mia.

Anonymous
Tu che accendi questo
Tu che accendi questo

201

Cinti-Damoreau II
rem- plir mon â- me
[il va- lor mi- o,]

(Anon.)
co- re tu che des- ti il va- lor mi- o al- ma
co- re, tu che des- ti il va- lor mi- o, al- ma

m'en- flam- me- re, ton feu m'a-
[-ce a- mo- re,] se- con-
glo- ria Dol- ce a- mo- re Se- con-

Gregoire
-mo- re Se- con-

glo- ria, dol- ce a- mo- re, se- con-

Pasta
il bel de- si- o
(CD II)
-gi- te il m'en flam- me
-da- te il bel de- si- o,]
(Anon.)
-da- te il bel de- si- o Ca- da un
(Greg.)
-da- te il bel de- si- o Ca- da un'
fm
60
-da- te il bel de- si- o, ca- da un
Pasta
co- ro-
autre
[oui]
[co- ro-
Cinti-Damoreau II
oui ce
[co- ro-
(Anon.)
em- pio tra- di- to- re co- ro-
(Greg.)
em- pio tra- di- to- re co- ro-
a piacere
em- pio tra- di- to- re, co- ro-
sf
colla parte

(Pasta)
-na- te il mio va-
(CD II autre)
-na- te il mio vain- queur
va- lor.]
(CD II)
bras se- ra vain- queur
na- te il mio va- lor.]
(Anon.)
-na- te il mio va- lor
(Greg.)
a piacere
-na- te co- ro- na- te il mio va- lor
-na- te la mia fé.
a tempo
Moderato
65
stacc.
70
Di tan- ti pal- pi- ti,
stacc.

Anonymous
tan- te
6
be- ne spe- ro mer-
75
3 3
di tan- te pe- ne, da te mio be- ne, spe- ro mer-
80
striscriata
85
-cé. Mi ri- ve- dra- i . . . ti ri- ve- drò,
p
Cinti-Damoreau II
[3] [3]
char- me mes yeux ob-
[ti ri- ve- drò. . . .]
Anonymous
ti ri- ve- dró ra- i
90
ti ri- ve- drò . . . ne' tuoi bei rai
pp stacc.

(CD II) -jet de mes feux [mi pa-sce-rò.]   sans ces-se [ac-cen-ti,]

(Anon.) mi pa-sce-ró

Gregoire: mi pa-sce-ro o ca-ri mo-men-ti o dol-ci con-

mi pa-sce-rò. De-li-ri, so-spi-ri... ac-cen-ti, con-

Cinti-Damoreau II: fi-dè-le sans ces sc t'ap-
[so-spi-ri... ac-cen-ti, con-

Anonymous: so-spi-ri a-ven-ti con-

-ten-ti o ca-ri mo-men-ti o dol-ci con-

-ten-ti!...De-li-ri, so-spi-ri... ac-cen-ti, con-

206

(Anon.)
mi ri- ve- dra- i ti ri- ve- dró
(Greg.) mf
mi ri- ve- dra- i ti ri- ve- drò
110
strisciata
Mi ri- ve- dra- i . . . ti ri- ve- drò,
Cinti-Damoreau II
char- me mes yeux
[ti ri- ve- drò . . .]
Anonymous
ti ri- ve dró
Gregoire
ti ri- ve- drò
115
ti ri- ve- drò . . .
p
pp stacc.
(CD II)
que sa con- stan- ce com- ble mes
[ne' tuoi bei ra- i mi pa- sce-
(Anon.)
ne tuoi bei ra- i mi pa- sce-
(Greg.)
ne' tuoi bei ra- i mi pa- sce
ne' tuoi bei rai mi pa- sce-

(CD II)
voeux
-ro.]
Cinti-Damoreau II
que ta pré-
[ne' tuoi bei
(Anon.)
-ró mi ri- ve- dra- i ti ri- ve- dró ne' tuoi bei
120
-rò. Mi ri- ve- dra- i . . . ti ri- ve- drò . . . ne' tuoi bei
stacc.
-sen- ce char- me mes yeux
ra- i mi pa- sce- ro.]
ra- i mi pa- sce- ró
125
ra- i mi pa- sce- rò. Mi ri- ve- dra- i . . . ti ri- ve-
Cinti-Damoreau II
-fian- ce que ta pré- sen- ce char-me mes yeux que
[-drò . . . ne' tuoi bei ra- i mi pa-sce- rò, mi
Anonymous
-dró ne tuoi bei ra- i mi pa-sce- ro mi
Gregoire
-dro ne tuoi bei ra- i mi pa- sce- rò ne' tuoi bei
-drò . . . ne' tuoi bei ra- i mi pa-sce- rò, mi
f
pp

(CD II) ta pré- sen- ce mi char- me pa- mes sce-

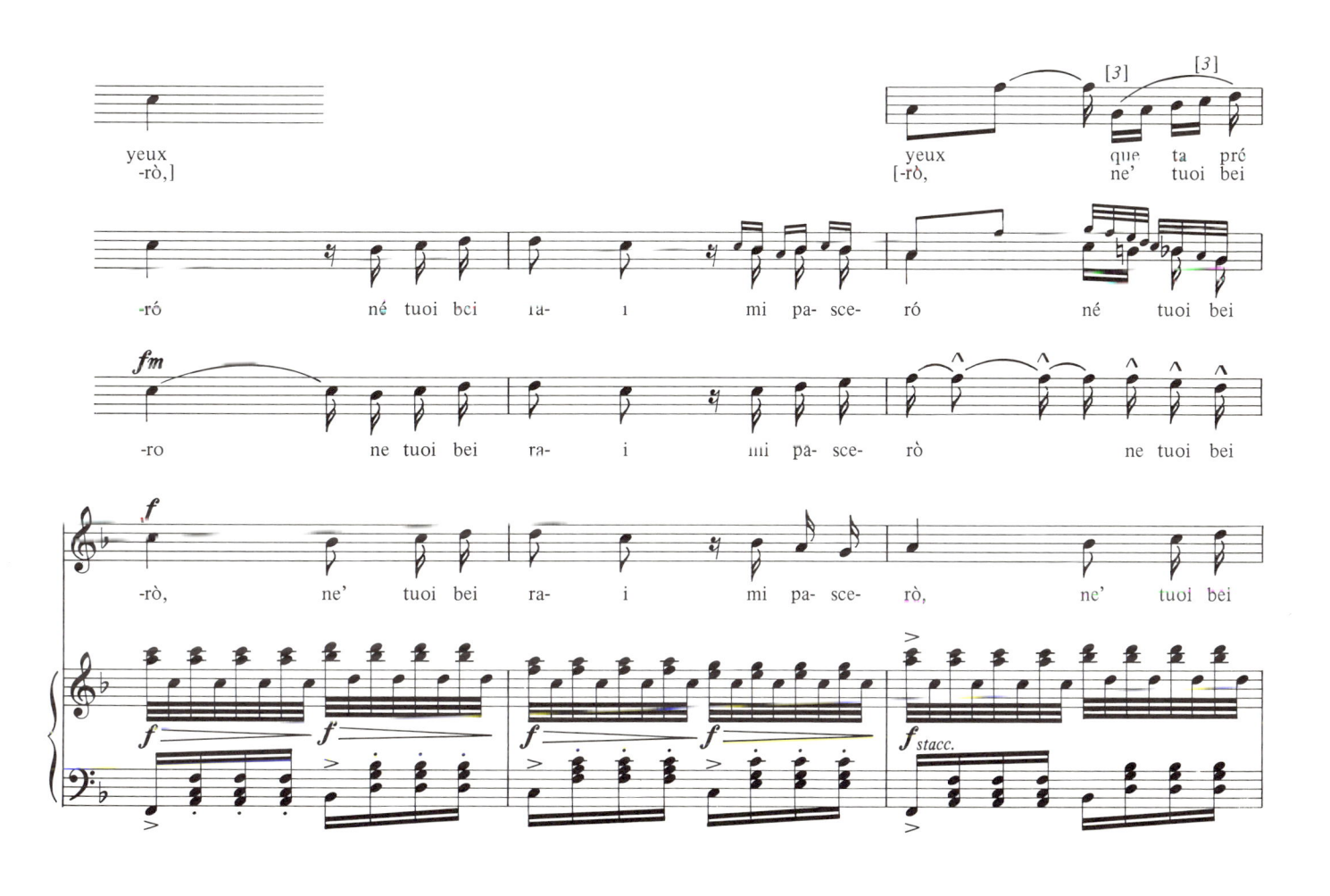

(Anon.) pa- sce- ró mi pa- sce-

(Greg.) rai mi pa- sce- ro ne tuoi bei rai mi pa- sce-

pa- sce- rò, mi pa- sce-

yeux [-rò,] yeux que ta pré
-ró né tuoi bei ra- i mi pa- sce- ró né tuoi bei
-ro ne tuoi bei ra- i mi pa- sce- rò ne tuoi bei
-rò, ne' tuoi bei ra- i mi pa- sce- rò, ne' tuoi bei

(CD II)
-sen- ce char- me mes yeux char- me mes yeux char- me mes
ra- i mi pa- sce- rò, mi pa- sce- rò, mi pa- sce-
(Anon.)
ra- i mi pa- sce- ró mi pa- sce-
(Greg.)
ra- i mi pa- sce- rò mi pa- sce- rò [mi pa- sce-]
135
rai mi pa- sce- rò, mi pa- sce- rò, mi pa- sce-
f
yeux char- me mes yeux
-rò, mi pa- sce- rò.]
ró mi [3] pa- sce- ró.
fmo
3
-ro mi pa- sce- rò.
140
-rò, mi pa- sce- rò.
f

[22] Lasciami: non t'ascolto
(*Tancredi*)

Gioachino Rossini

Pasta

Lasciami non t'ascolto non t'ascolto [se-]

Allegro giusto
TANCREDI

Lasciami: non t'ascolto, non t'ascolto: se-

-durmi in van, in van tu speri que' sguardi

-durmi in van tu speri: que' sguardi

lusinghieri serba serba al novelo a-

lusinghieri serba, serba al novelo a-

-mor se- dur- mi in- van tu spe- ri quei
-mor, se- dur- mi in- van tu spe- ri: que'
sguar- di lu- sin- ghie- ri ser- ba al no- vel- lo a-
sguar- di lu- sin- ghie- ri ser- ba al no- vel- lo a-
-mor quei sguar- di lu- sin- ghie- ri
-mor, que' sguar- di lu- sin- ghie- ri
ser- ba al no- vel- lo a-
ser- ba al no- vel- lo a-

AMENAIDE: O-dimi: e poi m'uccidi, e poi m'uccidi: sì, che innocente io sono: riprenditi il tuo dono, se rea, se rea, se rea mi credi ancor, sì, che innocente sono: riprenditi il tuo dono, se rea mi credi an-

(Pasta) -mor.

-cor, ri- pren- di- ti il tuo do- no, se rea mi cre- di an-

-cor.

colla parte

f a tempo   *pp*

Andantino

TANCREDI

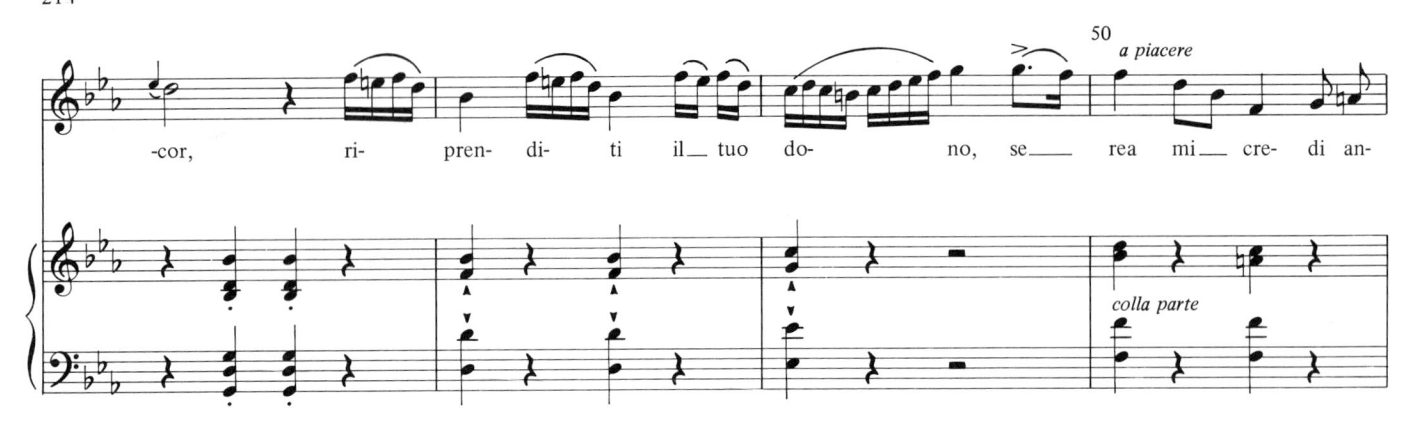

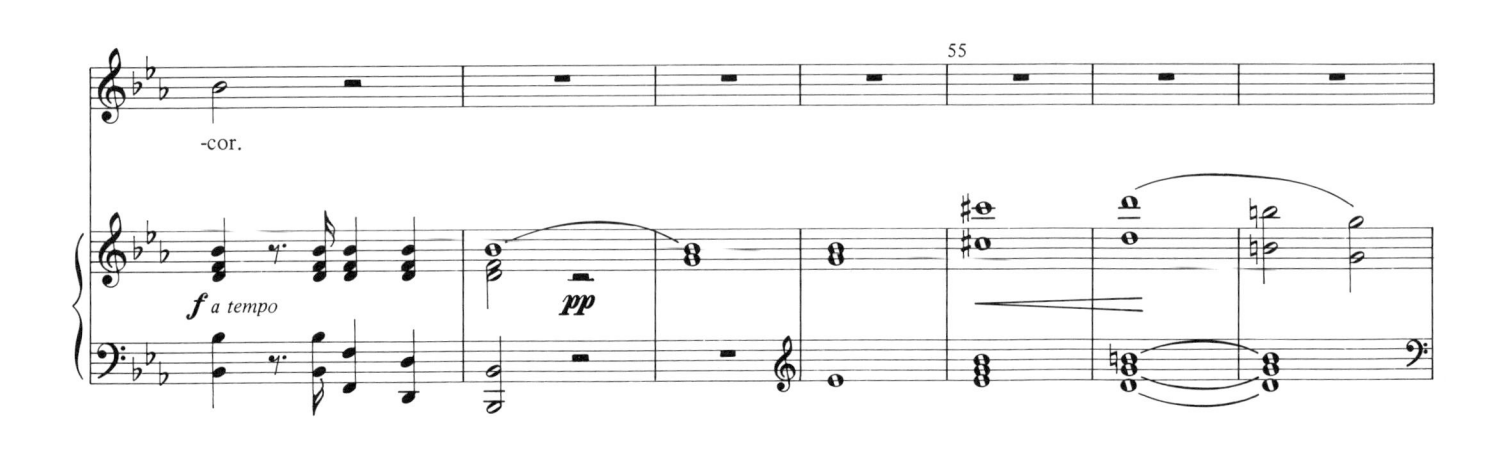

Ah! co- me mai quel- l'a- ni- ma can-

pp   *stacc.*

-giò per me d'af- fet- to! Per chi so- spi- ri in pet- to, o

AMENAIDE
Ah! che fe-del que- st'a- ni-ma ser- bò il giu-ra- to af-
de- bo-le mio cor? Per chi
-fet- to. . . . Fo- sti tu sol l'og- get- to del
so- spi- ri, o mio
te- ne- ro mio cor. Ah! che fe- del que- st'a- ni-ma ser-
cor? Ah! co- me mai quel- l'a- ni-ma can- giò per me d'af-
strisciata
-bò il giu- ra- to af- fet- to. . . . Fo- sti tu sol l'og- get- to,
-fet- to, can- giò! Per chi so- spi- ri in pet- to,

85
fo- sti tu sol l'og- get- to del te- ne- ro mio cor,
per chi so- spi- ri in pet- to, o de- bo- le mio cor,
del te- ne- ro mio cor. Fo- sti tu sol l'og-
o de- bo- le mio cor? Per chi so- spi- ri in
stacc.
90
-get- to, fo- sti tu sol l'og- get- to,
pet- to, per chi so- spi- ri in pet- to,
95
del te- ne- ro mio cor, del te- ne- ro mio
o de- bo- le mio cor, o de- bo- le mio

217

cor, del tenero mio cor, del

cor, o debole mio cor, o

Cinti-Damoreau III

tenero [tenero mio cor]

debole debole mio

tenero mio

debole mio

mio cor.

mio cor?

Allegro

110
Dun-que?
La- sciar- mi puo- i?
Ad- di- o.
Che più
pp dolce
f
115
Se- guir- ti.
E qui
vuo- i? . . .
Tre- ma, tre- ma.
ff
120
sfo- ga il tuo fu- ro- - re.
sf
sf
sf

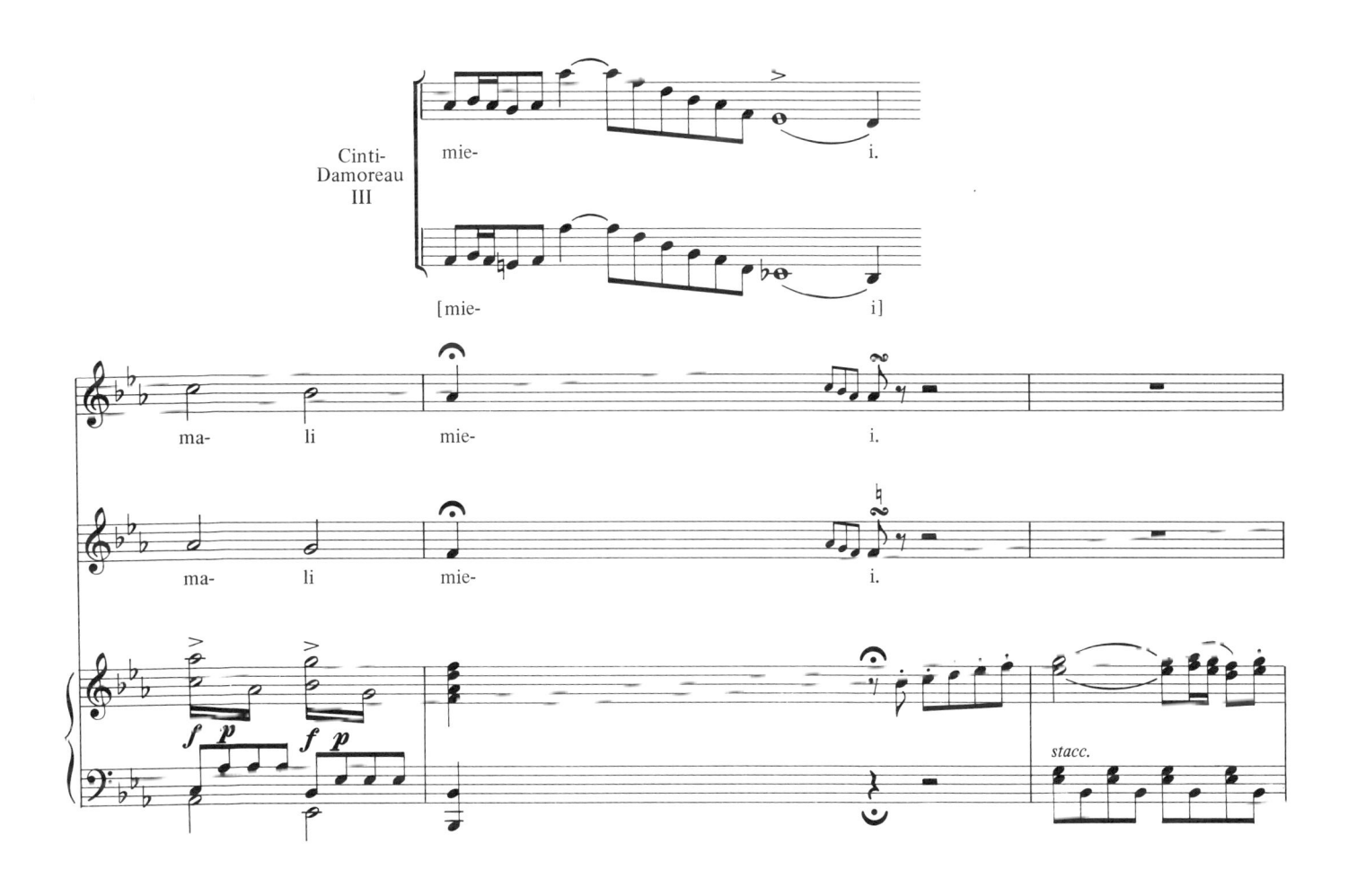

*This edition cuts from m. 133 to m. 221 (see Critical Notes).

M2.R23834 v.7-8 Q

Embellished opera arias.